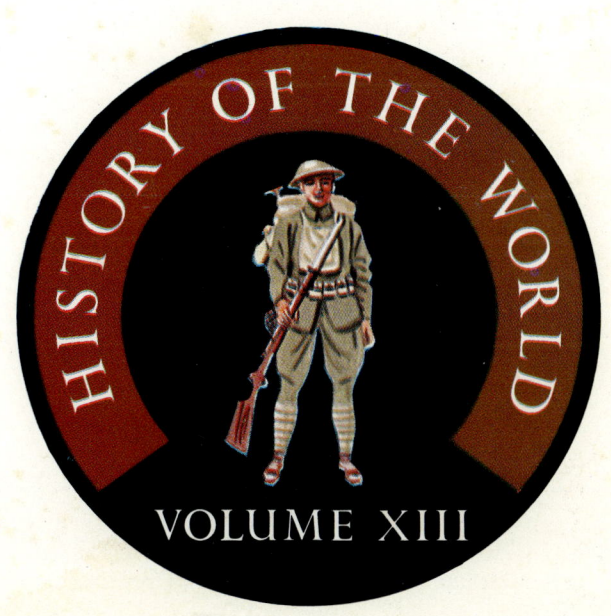

IMPORTANT DATES AND EVENTS —

The Museum of Modern Art, N.Y.

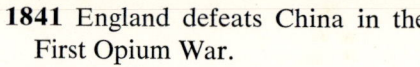

1841 England defeats China in the First Opium War.
1853 Perry visits Japan.
1854 Perry returns to Japan and signs a treaty opening two ports to American ships.
1856 The Second Opium War; English and French win special rights in China.
1857 The Sepoy Revolt is put down and England consolidates her rule in India.
1865 With the end of the Civil War, the United States begins to industrialize rapidly.
1866 Completion of the transatlantic telegraph cable.
1867 Japan is reformed by the emperor and begins to industrialize.
1869 The Suez Canal in Egypt and the transcontinental railway in America are completed, opening new markets to industry.
1871 Prussia unifies Germany, becoming the German Empire.
1875 England buys a controlling interest in the Suez Canal.
1876 Bell invents the telephone.
1877 Russia conquers several Turkish provinces.

IMPERIALISM AND WORLD WAR I, 1841-1898

1878 The Congress of Berlin keeps peace in Europe by giving the powers parts of Turkey.
1882 Germany, Austria-Hungary, and Italy form the Triple Alliance, pledging to aid each other in case of war; Leopold of Belgium acquires the Congo; Egypt becomes a British protectorate.
1883 France takes Annam from China and combines it with other colonies to form Indochina.
1884 The Berlin conference recognizes the Congo and sets up standards for African colonies.
1894 Japan seizes Korea from China; France and Russia form the Dual Alliance.
1895 The Boers repel the Jameson raid in the Transvaal.
1896 The kaiser congratulates Kroger of the Transvaal on the defeat of Jameson; great indignation in England.
1898-1901 The Boer War.
1898 British and French forces meet at Fashoda in Africa; war between Spain and the U.S.; the U.S. conquers Puerto Rico and the Philippines and annexes Hawaii.

HISTORY OF

Editor	Irwin Shapiro
Associate Editor	Jonathan Bartlett
Consultant	Albert Fried, *Department of History, Queens College, New York*
Contributors	Anne Howard Bailey
	John Bowman
	Ormonde de Kay, Jr.
	Edith Firoozi
	Albert Fried
	Johanna Johnston
	Ira N. Klein
	Willis Lindquist
	Edna Ritchie
	Seymour Reit
	James L. Steffensen

VOLUME XIII

THE UNIVERSAL
THE WORLD

IMPERIALISM AND WORLD WAR I

by Ormonde de Kay, Jr.

GOLDEN PRESS　　NEW YORK

CONTENTS

Stepping-Stones for the West 1869   1041
The Suez Canal and the railway across America open new markets to industry.

Industry Transforms America 1865-1914   1043
After the Civil War, the United States becomes a great industrial power.

Problems of a Changing World 1870-1914   1049
The industrial countries race to acquire colonies for raw materials and markets.

The Race For Empire 1870-1914   1053
Inventions and the rise of trade unions bring changes to the industrial nations.

India and the Indies 1856-1914   1055
After the Sepoy Revolt, England consolidates her rule in India.

The Powers Carve Up China 1841-1914   1059
The European powers take advantage of the weakness of the Manchu emperors to gain special trading rights in China. Sun Yat-Sen founds the Republic of China.

Japan Meets the West 1853-1905   1062
Japan responds to the threat from the West by modernizing and industrializing the country. Japan defeats tsarist Russia in a war caused by rivalry in China.

Parceling Out a Continent 1841-1910   1067
England, France, Belgium and Germany compete for colonies in Africa.

© COPYRIGHT 1966 BY WESTERN PUBLISHING COMPANY, INC., AND LIBRAIRIE HACHETTE. ALL RIGHTS RESERVED INCLUDING THE RIGHT OF REPRODUCTION IN WHOLE OR IN PART IN ANY FORM. DESIGNED AND PRODUCED BY ARTISTS AND WRITERS PRESS, INC. PRINTED IN THE U.S.A. BY WESTERN PRINTING AND LITHOGRAPHING COMPANY. PUBLISHED BY GOLDEN PRESS, INC., NEW YORK.

Rivalries in the Middle East 1856-1912 — 1072
With the decline of the Ottoman Empire, the European powers compete for dominance in the Middle East.

The United States and Destiny 1848-1914 — 1074
The United States expands to the Pacific and defeats Spain to acquire the Philippines and Puerto Rico. Roosevelt begins construction of the Panama Canal.

Storm Clouds Over Europe 1882-1907 — 1080
The great powers form systems of alliances to maintain the balance of power.

The Coming of the Storm 1905-1913 — 1083
Germany builds its navy and tries to win colonies while Russia attempts to expand into the Balkans and gain a warm-water port.

The Storm Breaks 1914 — 1085
Serbian nationalists assassinate Archduke Ferdinand of Austria. Austria declares war on Serbia, and the alliance system pulls the other great powers into the war.

Stalemate in the West, Decision in the East 1914-1917 — 1088
The first German assault in France bogs down and trench warfare begins. The tsar is overthrown and the Bolsheviks make peace with Germany.

The United States and Victory 1915-1918 — 1102
A German submarine sinks the Lusitania *with over 100 Americans on board. The United States enters the war. Germany asks an armistice when it becomes clear that the war cannot be won. End of World War I.*

The Victors Reconstruct Europe 1918-1919 — 1116
The peace conference in Paris blames the war on Germany and imposes severe penalties. Austria-Hungary is broken up into several small countries. The powers found the League of Nations.

After the Peace of Paris 1919-1920 — 1122
War reparations disrupt the German economy and cause great discontent with the Versailles treaty. The U.S. Senate rejects the treaty and refuses to join the League.

IMPERIALISM AND WORLD WAR I

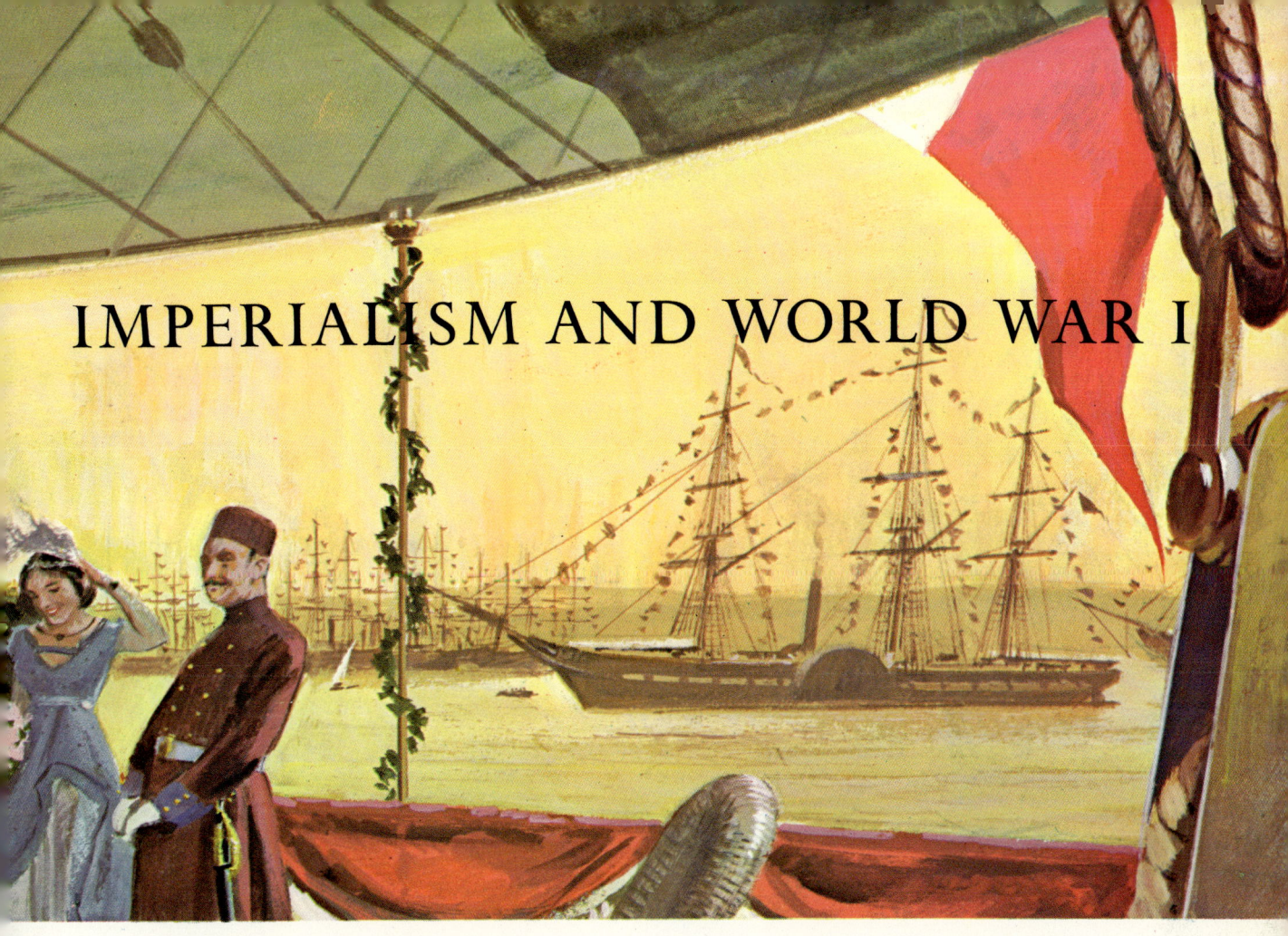

EMPRESS EUGENIE WELCOMED GUESTS AT THE OPENING OF THE SUEZ CANAL.

Stepping-Stones for the West
1869

ON NOVEMBER 16, 1869, the sun rose over the eastern end of the Mediterranean Sea and shone on the blue water. The squat buildings of Port Said, on the shore of Egypt, glowed against the clear sky. A new town, Port Said had begun to rise only ten years before from the barren plain that joins Africa to Asia.

In the man-made harbor were crowded eighty ships. Some were warships, others merchantmen, but all were strung with brightly-colored pennants. On board were distinguished visitors, among them the emperor of Austria-Hungary, the crown prince of Prussia, the prince of Holland, and ambassadors, generals, and admirals from many lands. As the sun climbed higher, passengers began to appear on the decks, and hundreds of other people gathered on the piers and the seawall.

At eight o'clock, the warships' big guns boomed out salutes to the European monarchs, to the khedive of Egypt, and to the khedive's overlord, the sultan of Turkey. When the smoke cleared, a trim, graceful vessel came steaming toward the harbor—the French imperial yacht *Aigle*. Again the cannon thundered, to welcome Empress Eugénie, the wife of Napoleon III. She was the guest of honor, and as her yacht glided past, the sailors on the other ships stood at attention, cheering, while music blared from several bands. The black-haired empress, standing on the *Aigle's* bridge, smiled to left and right. She looked happy and proud, and by the time her yacht had docked, everyone agreed she was as beautiful as she was said to be.

1041

Stepping-Stones for the West

In the afternoon, the visitors, in uniforms, frock coats, and formal gowns, and Egyptians, who wore flowing robes, all trooped out onto the desert. There, perhaps for the first time, Christians and Moslems worshiped side by side. The Moslems were led in prayer by the ulema, or religious chief, of Egypt, the Christians by the patriarch of Jerusalem. Then the Catholic priest who was Eugénie's confessor addressed the crowd. He thanked God for granting success to the project whose completion they were now celebrating. He thanked the empress and the other rulers present for supporting the project. Finally, he spoke of the tall, gray-haired man seated next to Eugénie—Ferdinand de Lesseps. It was thirty years since de Lesseps had first suggested building a canal from the Mediterranean to the Red Sea. He had faced many difficulties in promoting his plan, including the opposition of the powerful British government. But he had refused to be discouraged, and now, at last, the canal was a reality.

After sunset, fireworks blazed over Port Said, lighting up the night sky. The next morning, Eugénie and de Lesseps, on board the *Aigle,* led a file of ships south through the canal to the Red Sea port of Suez. The three-day trip went off smoothly, with stopovers for balls and fireworks displays, and everyone was delighted with the new waterway.

The Suez Canal shortened the sea distance between Europe and Asia by thousands of miles. Before it was opened, ships going from one continent to the other had had to sail all the way around Africa; and the voyage had taken at least six weeks. Now it took only three weeks or less. Although the British had opposed the canal, fearing that it would give the French too much control over trade with the Orient, they began to sail through it themselves on their way to and from India and the other British colonies on the Indian Ocean.

Ships using the canal paid tolls to the canal company, and as receipts mounted, the French financiers who had backed de Lesseps began to talk about building another great interoceanic canal in the other hemisphere. It would cut across the Isthmus of Panama, which connected North America to South America. It would link the Atlantic and Pacific oceans, and do away with the long sea voyage around Cape Horn, at the tip of South America. But Panama, with its mountains, jungles, and fever-ridden swamps, was a much more difficult place to build a canal than the flat and open Isthmus of Suez. Even the most enthusiastic promoters of the Panama canal admitted that it would take many years and huge amounts of money to complete.

Meanwhile, north of Panama, a different kind of link between oceans had been built in the

SHIPS OF ALL THE EUROPEAN NATIONS CONVERGED ON SUEZ FOR THE CEREMONY.

FACTORIES AND RAILROADS WERE BUILT ALONG THE RIVERS OF NEW ENGLAND.

United States—a transcontinental railway. On May 10, 1869, in the desert near Promontory, Utah, railway officials in top hats and frock coats had hammered down a golden spike to unite the tracks running toward it from east and west, while a crowd of workmen cheered. It was a simpler ceremony than the one which opened the Suez Canal six months later, but the event it marked was almost as important. Thanks to the new railway, people and goods could travel from one American coast to the other, and to points between, much faster and more safely than before.

The opening of the transcontinental railway and the Suez Canal in the same year showed how the world was changing. Although these two new links between oceans were thousands of miles apart they had been brought into being by the same force: the need of industry to reach out to distant lands for supplies and customers. Until the middle of the nineteenth century, industry had mostly been confined to the British Isles, where the Industrial Revolution had begun. At about that time, however, the Industrial Revolution spread to the other countries of northwestern Europe and to the northeastern part of the United States. By 1869, industry was thriving in these two regions, which faced each other across the Atlantic.

During the next forty-five years, industry's ever-growing demand for supplies and customers would make the nations of the West reach farther and farther outward, by land and sea. The Suez Canal and the transcontinental railway were both steppingstones in this direction. Before long the West would dominate the whole world with its military and financial might, its advanced technology, and its system of strong national governments. But, as competition among the industrial powers mounted, national rivalries would become ever sharper and more intense. In the end, these rivalries were to split the West apart and bring about a war more terrible than any the world had yet known.

Industry Transforms America

1865-1914

VETERANS OF the Union Army, returning to their home towns in New England or the Middle Atlantic states after the war, were surprised at what they saw. They had grown up in towns where most of the people lived by farming, while

1043

the rest sold things to farmers or worked in local workshops. Perhaps a mill and a factory had stood on the bank of the town's river. The farms, stores, and workshops remained, but now there were many new brick buildings used for factories, mills, and warehouses.

American industry, concentrated in the river valleys and ocean ports of the northeast, had grown with a rush during the Civil War. Behind the fighting lines, factories had turned out rails and telegraph wires, rifles and bullets, boots, uniforms, blankets, tents—all the articles needed for the Union forces. And these products of Northern industry made a big difference on the battlefields.

Before the war, the South had been an agricultural land, with large plantations worked by slaves and smaller farms worked by poor white farmers. Cotton was the big crop, and great quantities of it were sold, especially to the mills of Great Britain. The wealth of the South, based on the unpaid labor of slaves, had given it as much influence within the nation as the North, which was partly agricultural and partly industrial. But the South had little industry. When war came, it was unable to keep its fighting men supplied with weapons and other needs. The ill-equipped Southerners were worn down by the well-equipped Northerners, until finally they were completely defeated.

The victory of the Union upset the balance of power between the North and the South. With the freeing of the slaves, most of the Southern planters were ruined, while the leaders of industry in the North were stronger than ever. They included manufacturers, bankers, financiers, and company promoters, and owners of the railways which now criss-crossed the Northeast and stretched out over the flat and rolling farmlands of the Middle West.

Wealth and their control of industry and transportation made these men the most powerful in America. They dominated a dozen or more states, through lawmakers and government officials who did their bidding, and often they dominated the national government itself. They and the big businessmen who came after them were to play commanding roles in politics, setting government policy and picking men to fill high positions in government, throughout the next half-century of swift industrial growth.

In Boston, New York, Philadelphia, and other centers of industry, the end of the Civil War brought government orders to a sudden stop. Factory wheels slowed down. Soon, however, they were spinning as fast as ever, for the nation, once more united, needed their products in peace as it had in war. Farmers needed plows, wagons, and farm tools; miners needed spades and pickaxes; carpenters needed saws, hammers, and nails —and so on through all the trades and professions. And almost everybody wanted inexpensive, factory-made clothes in the latest fashion, as well as furniture, crockery, glassware, cutlery, and hardware.

SETTLERS AND IMMIGRANTS

As the country developed, so did its needs. New devices like the McCormick reaper, the sewing machine, and the typewriter were eagerly bought up when they came on sale. To turn out the goods people wanted, manufacturers had to have more and better machines. And so industry kept growing, slowly changing the lives of all Americans.

Even with the ever-increasing demand, the businessmen who made and sold goods would not have prospered as they did without the help of their friends and henchmen in government. Their products had to compete with products from other countries, especially Great Britain, which were often cheaper. To limit this competition, the national government put an import tax, or tariff, on manufactured goods coming into the country. This forced foreign manufacturers to raise their prices in the United States; to make a profit, they had to charge more for their wares than American manufacturers. As a result, sales of American goods went up and sales of foreign goods dropped.

Many Americans, especially farmers in the South, Middle West, and West, would have preferred no tariff and cheaper foreign goods. But most Americans, including the increasing number of industrial workers, favored the tariffs. The Republican party, which supported high tariffs, won election after election over the Democratic party, which supported free trade. Except for a comparatively few years, the Republicans controlled the national government from the time of the Civil War until just before World War I.

THE McCORMICK REAPER HELPED MAKE LARGE-SCALE FARMING POSSIBLE.

While the government protected industry from foreign competition, it also encouraged industrialists to extend their operations westward. It offered huge tracts of land in the West to companies that would build railroads, dig mines, or cut down forests for timber. Like the tariff policy, the land-grant policy made it easier for business ventures to succeed by reducing their risks. A new railroad, for example, might carry little freight during its first years, but it could still make money by leasing the land it had acquired along its tracks to cattlemen or selling tracts of land to farmers. And there was always a chance that the land might contain gold, silver, or other valuable minerals.

Not all of the business ventures were as successful as the transcontinental railroad. Some failed, and others turned out to be frauds. There

1045

Industry Transforms America

were gold mines that yielded nothing but rock dust, and railroads that existed only in the imagination of the stockholders. But more succeeded than failed, and slowly the "Wild West" was tamed—to the profit of investors, most of them in the eastern states.

Meanwhile, settlers poured into the empty land. By 1912, when the admission of New Mexico and Arizona to the Union completed the pattern of states from coast to coast, the American West had thousands of miles of railroads. Towns and cities rose on the prairies and in the mountain valleys, on the shore of the Pacific and even on the desert. And the value of the products sent east to market—minerals and timber, meat and hides, wool, grain, and fruit—multiplied a thousand times.

As a matter of fact, all America grew after the Civil War. Between 1860 and 1910, the number of people increased from 30 million to 90 million, as ship after ship brought new arrivals from overseas. For industry needed men by the thousands, and American firms sent agents to Europe to find workers. The Europeans were willing to listen. Like the Americans, the number of Europeans was increasing rapidly. Europe, too, was becoming industrialized—but only in the west and northwest. Within this area, industry created new jobs that kept pace with the growing population. Elsewhere, however, there were not enough jobs to go around, and some Europeans were unemployed and hungry.

Other Europeans had different reasons for their discontent. Some disliked their rulers, or the form of government under which they lived. Some were poor but ambitious, and they longed to escape from a land where there were few opportunities for anyone who did not belong to a rich or noble family. In America, anyone discontented with his lot could pack up and try his luck in the West; in Europe, there was no good land open to settlers. For Europeans, the only frontier was the Atlantic Ocean, beyond which lay America, the vast "land of opportunity."

And so thousands of Europeans listened eagerly to the agents and accepted their offer of a free trip across the ocean with a job waiting for them on the other side. And those who wanted to go to America and look for a job on their own could buy steamship tickets at low

THIS CARTOON SATIRIZED THE WAVES OF IMMIGRANTS FROM EUROPE.

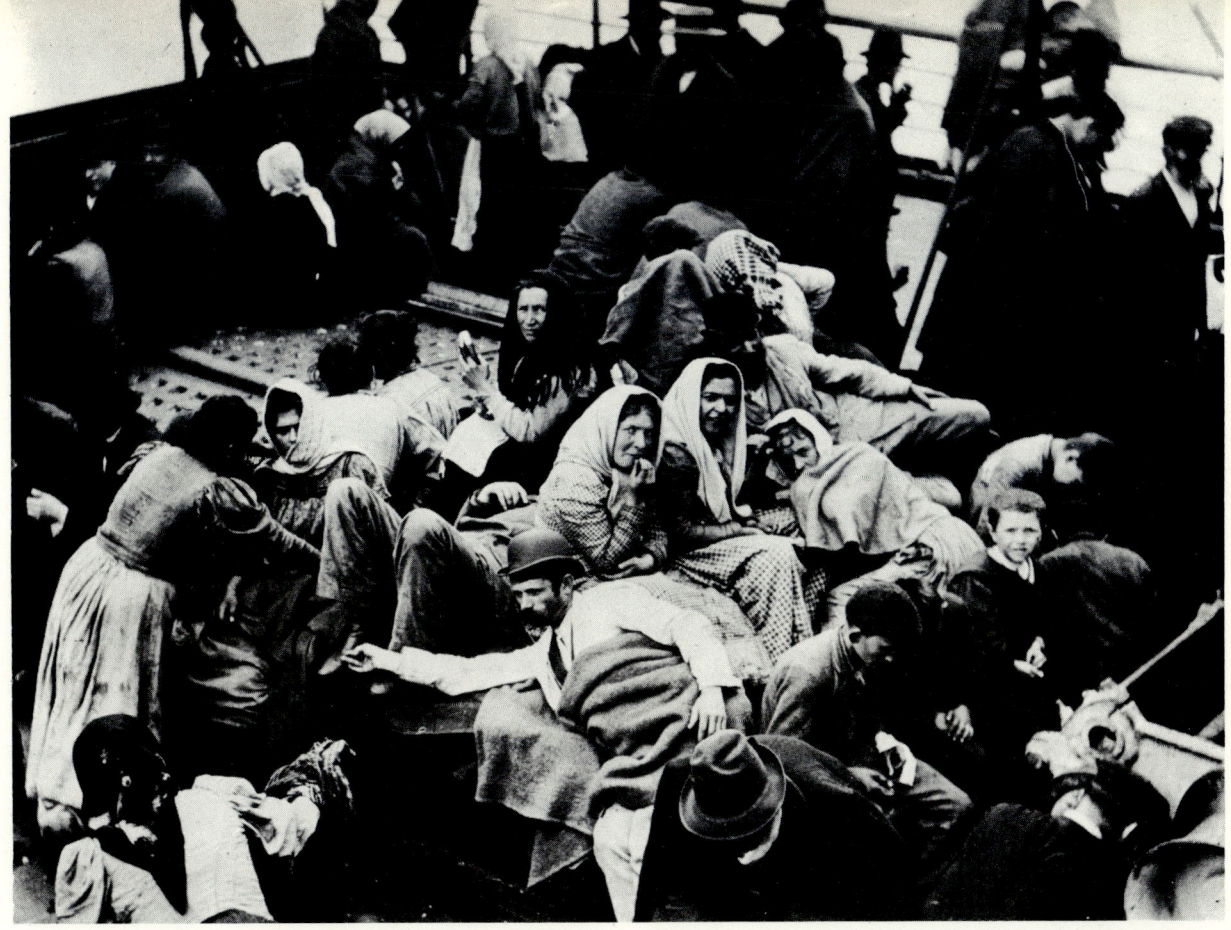

IMMIGRANTS CROWDED ABOARD SHIPS TO SEEK A NEW LIFE IN THE NEW WORLD.

rates. One way or another, millions of Europeans emigrated to America. Some went to Latin America or Canada, but the vast majority went to the United States. They usually landed in New York, where, after 1886, they were greeted by the giant Statue of Liberty. Almost all of them were poor, and they brought everything they owned with them, packed in trunks or boxes or simply wrapped in kerchiefs or pieces of cloth. After a short stay in the government receiving station on Ellis Island, they went ashore to discover the New World for themselves.

Often the newcomers were put to work at hard, heavy tasks that native-born Americans did not want. Many worked on construction gangs, erecting buildings and bridges and laying out roads and railways. The transcontinental railway, for instance, was mostly laid by Irishmen, working their way west from Missouri, and Chinese, working east from California.

The vast westward flow of human beings, the greatest migration in history, began in the 1840's, reached its peak in the first years of the twentieth century, and did not die out until the 1920's. The first waves of immigrants came from western and northern Europe, the later waves from eastern and southern Europe.

THE LAND OF OPPORTUNITY

In 1846, Ireland's potato crop was ruined by a blight; to escape the terrible famine that followed, more than a million Irish people came to America. Most were poor peasants with little schooling. By contrast, there were many professional men and skilled mechanics among the Germans who began to arrive after the liberal revolution of 1848 was put down. Later, Danes, Swedes, and Norwegians came, many of them settling on farms in the Middle West.

Begining around 1890, most of the newcomers were from Poland which was then under the rule of Russia. Among them were large numbers of Jews, fleeing from persecution. Within a few years they were followed by thousands of Italians leaving behind the poverty and overcrowding of their native land.

1047

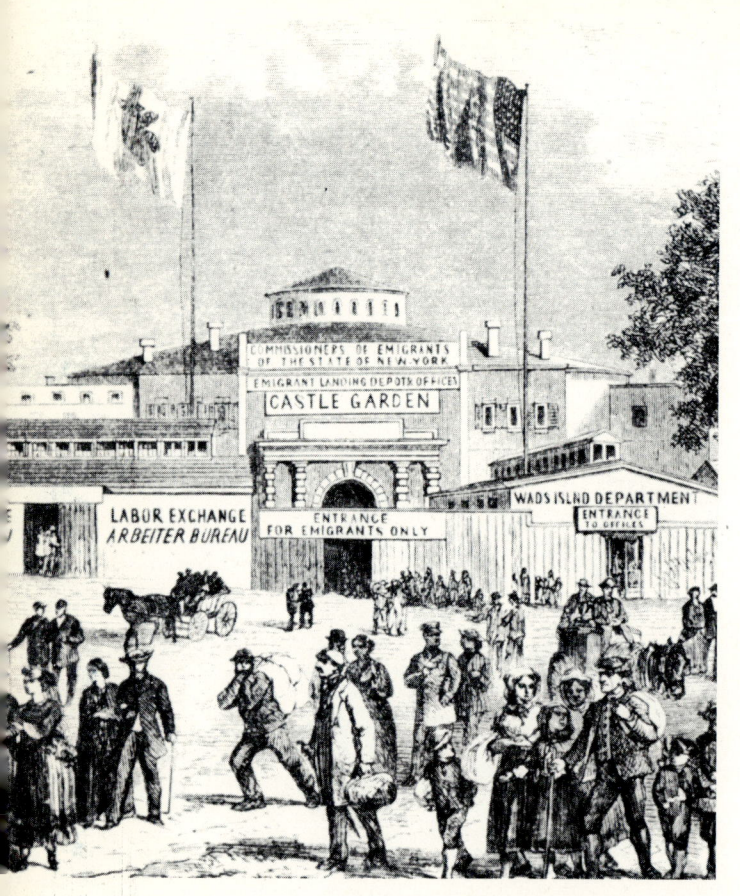

During the decade, or ten-year period, of 1840-1850, the number of immigrants was a million and three-quarters. During each of the next three decades, arrivals averaged about two and a half million, rising to five and a quarter million between 1880 and 1890. In the last decade of the nineteenth century only three and three-quarter million persons arrived, but the first ten years of the twentieth century brought a record-breaking nine million men, women, and children to the United States. Another ten million came between 1910 and the end of the 1920's, when a law curbing immigration turned the flood of arrivals into a mere trickle.

Almost all the immigrants settled in the North, the Middle West, and the West—that is, outside the southern states of the old Confederacy. While the great majority came from Europe, a small fraction came from China and Japan, and another small fraction from Canada and Latin America. In Europe, most of the immigrants had lived on the land; in the United States, most found work in towns and cities where industry was established, and stayed there. Meanwhile, more and more native-born Americans were leaving

ORIGINALLY A FORT, CASTLE GARDEN WAS FROM 1858 TO 1890 AN IMMIGRATION STATION FOR THOUSANDS OF NEW ARRIVALS LIKE THOSE BELOW.

the farms to take jobs in factories, stores, and offices, and the cities grew rapidly.

Between 1860 and 1910, the population of the country's largest city, New York, increased from 1,750,000 to 4,750,000. Chicago grew from a city of about 50,000 to a metropolis with a million and a half inhabitants. And Los Angeles, which had been no more than a village before the Civil War, became a city of half a million.

Even more significant was the rise in the proportion of city-dwellers to country-dwellers in the national population. In 1860, only one American in twelve lived in a town or city; by 1910, it was one in three. At the time of the Civil War, the United States was mainly a farming country, but during the next fifty years it became thoroughly industrialized. By the beginning of World War I, it was a great industrial power.

Problems of a Changing World
1870-1914

WHILE INDUSTRY was transforming the United States, the same thing was happening in Western Europe. The change was most noticeable in Germany. Because Germany was not unified until 1870, it started to become industrial much later than Great Britain and France, but it soon began to catch up with its neighbors. Within a few decades it was producing more than they were of several key commodities, including the most important one of all, steel.

Like the American government, the German government imposed tariffs on foreign manufactures, and encouraged its national industry in other ways. The results were much the same as in the United States. Railways spread across the country in an ever denser network of tracks, connecting farmlands with cities, mines with factories, and factories with seaports. New industrial cities came into being, especially in the coal-rich Ruhr Valley, next to the iron-rich province of Lorraine which Germany had seized from France in the Franco-Prussian War. And old cities doubled and tripled in size as country people flocked into them to man factory machines, shop counters, and office desks.

On both sides of the Atlantic, smoke billowed from factory chimneys, rows of new houses went up in the cities, and freight trains carried industrial products off to market—and to seaports, for shipments overseas. Such signs of industry's growth could be seen throughout the industrial West. Elsewhere, in the less developed parts of the world, they were not so evident—but their effects were felt just the same.

For, as industry expanded in Western Europe and the United States, it reached further and further afield in quest of supplies for its factories and customers for its products. In Asia, Africa, Latin America, and other non-industrial regions, armies of native workers came to depend for their livelihood on the money some distant European or American businessman paid their employer for the tin they mined or the cotton they picked or the raw rubber they collected. In turn, the same workers spent part of their wages on pots and pans, shirts and dresses, and other articles fashioned by distant machines out of the very materials they provided. Thus, through trade, peoples separated by oceans and continents —and by completely different ways of life—came into regular contact with one another.

This change, the most momentous of all the changes brought about by the rise of industry, took place over a mere half century. It could not have come about so quickly without the drive and determination of men who planned and built canals and railways, bridges, harbors, and drydocks, ships and locomotives. But what hastened the change even more was the work of inventors.

FARMING DECLINES

To meet the challenges raised by the growth of industry and trade, men of science throughout the West turned their talents to improving engines that made use of natural forces, such as the steam engine, and to devising new ones. Out of their experiments came faster, more powerful railway engines and ships that carried large cargoes at high speeds across thousands of miles. Meanwhile, other inventors were trying to solve the problem of communicating over long distances—a problem which became more and more pressing as world trade grew in value and vol-

Problems of a Changing World

FIELD WAS HONORED IN 1858 BUT HIS CABLE WAS UNRELIABLE UNTIL 1866.

ume. In 1866, an American named Cyrus Field laid the first successful telegraph cable across the Atlantic. Ten years later, another American, Alexander Graham Bell, invented the telephone. And in 1895, an Irish-Italian inventor, Guglielmo Marconi, sent radio signals through the air for the first time. These inventions and others were quickly improved.

The outcome of all this activity was a worldwide revolution in transportation and communications. By the start of the twentieth century, the time it took to travel to far-off places was half or even a third of what it had been only fifty years before. Soon, the automobile and the airplane would reduce travel time even further. And already it was possible to transmit commercial or other information half way around the globe in a twinkling.

To the people of the West, the world, which had seemed vast to their grandfathers and even to their fathers, appeared to have shrunk. Because of the commercial ties that bound the industrial countries ever more tightly to the non-industrial lands, events in remote places now directly affected the lives of the people in New York and London, Paris and Berlin. Few people anywhere still lived completely apart from the rest of humanity. The great sea and land barriers that had always divided mankind were no longer so important. For the first time, the history of the world had become the history of all its peoples together.

THE TRADE UNIONS

The industrial West was the heart of the world of the late nineteenth and early twentieth centuries; it received raw materials and pumped out a stream of products. The West thrived on the world-wide circulation of goods. In the United States and Western Europe, businessmen piled up fortunes. And, as new jobs were created, the standard of living rose for many people.

But not everyone shared in the new prosperity. Industrialism came at a price—a price paid, first of all, by the farmers. Attracted by jobs in factories and mills, young people were leaving the land. In Europe, furthermore, many families were leaving their farms for new homes overseas. Meanwhile, towns grew into cities, and cities became still larger. This meant that fewer farmers had to produce more food, using the new labor-saving farm machines turned out by industry.

The difficulty was that the farmers did not profit from having more customers. Industrial leaders, through their friends in government, saw to it that the food their workers ate stayed inexpensive. Competition from abroad also kept down the prices paid to farmers for their crops. As world trade increased, more and more ships steamed home with cargoes of food, especially grain and dried meat, from newly-opened lands like Australia, Argentina, and South Africa. In the United States, with its broad expanses of productive soil, large-scale farming remained profitable, but in Europe it became less and less so. Many farmers turned to raising fruit, vegetables, and dairy products instead of grain or cattle.

As farming declined, industry boomed, and the workers in the cities fared better than the farmers. Even so, their life was far from easy. They worked twelve hours a day, six days a week, in bleak and badly-lighted factories and mills. The machines they operated were dangerous: if an operator was not careful, one of his hands or arms might be crushed or cut off, or

Problems of a Changing World

INDUSTRIALIZATION CHANGED THE MEANING OF POWER. TINY ENGLAND'S LEAD IN SHIPPING AND HEAVY INDUSTRY MADE HER THE STRONGEST NATION IN EUROPE.

he might even be killed. Their wages were barely enough to keep their families alive. To make ends meet, many working class families put their children to work in the local mill or mine, sometimes when they were only six years old.

Slowly, however, the workers came to see that their employers needed them as much as they themselves needed their wages. They banded together in trade unions to bargain for more pay and better working conditions. The first unions organized skilled workers who followed a particular trade, such as carpentry. The craft unions which began to flourish in Great Britain in the 1850's were conservative and avoided open conflict with employers. By 1884, all British workers had received the right to vote.

In the 1880's, new and larger unions of unskilled workers came into being. Industrial unions, as they were called, aimed to take in all British workers within an industry, such as coal, steel, or transportation, no matter what jobs they held. Some older craft unions joined the new industrial unions. By 1900, Great Britain had about two million union members, compared to only 850,000 in Germany and 250,000 in France.

In the United States, too, labor began to organize. May Day, which soon became the international working men's holiday and later the principal holiday in Communist countries, was first celebrated by workmen in Philadelphia in 1881. But the union movement in America was fiercely resisted by employers, who were often backed

Problems of a Changing World

MEMBERS OF THE SOCIAL DEMOCRATIC PARTY DEMONSTRATED IN LONDON.

by local and state governments. This conflict between employers and workers sometimes led to violence, which scared off many workers and delayed public acceptance of the movement. Not until the twentieth century did American unions begin to gain a sure foothold.

The unions' chief weapon in every country was the strike. Bargaining with employers was usually friendly, but if an employer refused to grant demands which a union considered vital, the union leaders might forbid their members to work. The workers then went on strike; instead of wages, they received food or small handouts from union funds made up of the membership dues they had contributed. If the employer hired new workers who did not belong to the union, the striking workers would try to prevent them from entering his factory or mill. As union membership became ever more effective, sometimes the mere threat of a strike was enough to make an employer give in to his workers' demands.

Little by little, in Western Europe and the United States, pay and working conditions improved. By 1900, the working day in most industries had been reduced to ten hours. Safer machines had been introduced, and several countries had passed laws limiting or forbidding the employment of children. And the unions, regarded at first with fear by industrialists and governments alike, were beginning to be accepted as responsible and respectable institutions.

One reason for the change was the steady improvement of the machines and methods used in manufacturing. Workers could turn out more goods in less time, so that their employer could pay them more money for fewer hours of work and still make a profit. Another reason was that the workers were gaining political power. In the United States, working men already had the vote, but in most European countries only citizens with property could vote until the last third of the nineteenth century. After 1867, the countries of Europe followed the example of Britain and granted almost all citizens the right to vote. As voters, workers could put pressure on their governments to bring about the changes they wanted.

THE SOCIALISTS

In Europe, many workers supported the economic doctrine known as socialism. Socialism came from several sources and took various forms, but after about 1880 it was based mainly on the ideas of Karl Marx, a German writer and teacher who had lived for many years in exile in London. Socialists believed, like Marx, that the means of production, such as farms, factories, tools, and machines, and the means of distribution, such as railways, ships, stores, and shops, should belong to the workers rather than to the businessmen and stockholders who profited from them. Because the existing economic system was based on capital—that is, money invested in business for profit—they called it capitalism.

The socialists wanted to replace capitalism with their own system. They founded political parties in democratic countries and began to explain their doctrine and recruit members, especially among industrial workers. In nondemocratic countries like Russia, they founded undercover socialist movements.

From the start, the socialists were split into two camps, which agreed on aims but disagreed strongly on the methods of attaining them. In the democratic countries of the West, socialism was evolutionary: its leaders wanted to come to power peacefully by electing enough socialists to take over the government. But in nondemocratic countries, whose rulers ruthlessly strove to stamp out the movement, socialism was revolutionary. Revolutionary socialists saw capitalism not as a rival to be overcome by votes, but as an enemy to be overthrown by force. This militant brand of socialism was also called communism, after the brief and bloody attempt to set up a workers' government in the Paris Commune of 1871.

Evolutionary socialism rapidly gained followers in the advanced industrial countries of continental Europe, especially France, Germany, and Belgium. There, socialists controlled the unions, and many socialists were elected to the national law-making bodies. Although no socialist party succeeded in winning control of a government, the socialists in the national parliaments were numerous enough to influence government policy. The evolution to socialism which businessmen dreaded did not take place, but many socialist proposals were adopted, further easing the lot of workers and poor citizens. The German socialists were particularly successful, and in Germany a broad program of social benefits was written into law.

Socialism had few followers in the United States, where it was easier to acquire property and set up small businesses than in Europe. Most Americans looked on socialism as something foreign, and the American Socialist party remained weak in numbers and strength. Socialist ideas, however, strongly influenced the "grass-roots" movement of farmers and laborers known as Populism, which flourished in the Middle West and West and reached a peak of political strength early in the twentieth century.

In Great Britain, too, socialism made little headway. Although the British unions were much stronger, richer, and more firmly established than those of any other country, they were also more conservative. British working men had no political tradition, and tended to resist new ideas, especially if they came from abroad. For years, union leaders and members alike remained indifferent to socialism.

Meanwhile, however, socialist ideas gained favor among liberal-minded men and women of the middle class and even the upper class. In 1906, the Labor Party was founded, on a program of socialist principles. Gradually the working class and the labor unions came to support the Labor party. Thereafter, control of the party remained mostly in the hands of union leaders. Thus, in Great Britain, the unions dominated the socialists, while on the continent the socialists dominated the unions.

The Race For Empire
1870-1914

While the peoples of the West were concerned with the problems that grew out of industrialization, their governments were taking part in one of the greatest land grabs in history. By the end of the nineteenth century they had brought within their grasp most of the earth's land surface and half its inhabitants. Because this development created new empires and enlarged old ones, it was called imperialism.

Imperialism came about in many ways, from armed invasions to polite talks that led native rulers to place their countries under the protection of an imperialist power. It took many forms, from colonies which one power ruled outright, to "spheres of influence," in which one power

FOREIGN TRADING POSTS LINED THE WATERFRONT OF CANTON, CHINA.

enjoyed rights, particularly trading rights, denied to other powers. And it arose from many causes—economic, political, and cultural.

Empire-building was not new; it was as old as civilization. In ancient times, the Romans had built a vast empire that ruled peoples in Europe, Asia and Africa. In the fifteenth century, European nations had colonized the Americas and conquered the Indians. But elsewhere they had not challenged native rulers, being content to set up trading posts, where they bought native wares for resale at home.

In the last quarter of the eighteenth century, most of British North America became independent, as did the United States. In the first quarter of the nineteenth century, almost all of Latin America won its freedom from Spain and Portugal. During the next half-century, while industry went through its first slow stage of growth, goods circulated freely throughout the world, and governments cared little about building up their empires. The French, to be sure, occupied Algeria, the British strengthened their hold on India, the Dutch developed the East Indies, and the western powers, including the United States, opened Japan to trade and started to penetrate China. But the powers made no great effort to enlarge their overseas domains.

About 1870, a change set in. Industrialists demanded that their governments protect them with tariffs. Soon, of all the powers of first rank, only Great Britain remained true to free trade and the doctrine that goods should be allowed to cross frontiers without being taxed. In the other industrial countries, tariffs encouraged industry to grow, but at the same time made it harder for manufacturers in any one country to sell their products in the others. And even though the demand for goods in each country kept growing along with its population and wealth, businessmen still had more goods to sell than their countrymen could buy. They began to look to lands outside Europe for customers.

Furthermore, manufacturers everywhere wanted to be sure of getting raw materials when they needed them and in large enough quantities. They and the other businessmen who had grown rich from industry were also eager for opportunities to invest their spare cash in ventures which would bring them bigger profits than their investments at home, at the lowest possible risk. And so governments were under pressure to take over undeveloped lands and safeguard them with soldiers. Before long, a race for empire was under way among the great powers.

THE WHITE MAN'S BURDEN

In this race, the leaders were the foremost industrial powers—Great Britain, France, and Germany. The first two, already possessing empires, had a head start on the third. Behind the leaders came three old colonial powers, Spain,

1054

Portugal, and Holland, and a small new industrial power, Belgium. Last to enter the race were two newly industrialized countries, Italy and Japan, and the United States.

The imperialist race began as a contest for a greater share of the world market. Quite soon, however, economic rivalry got mixed up with political rivalry. It came to be a matter of prestige, involving the pride of its citizens, for a power to possess land overseas, even if that land was nothing but barren mountains or desert. Many empires, in fact, cost far more to maintain than they yielded in profits.

Taking over land meant taking over the people who lived there, and this disturbed some Europeans. Was it right, they asked, to conquer natives, armed only with spears and blowguns, and then force them to clear and till plantations, build railways, and dig mines—all for the enrichment of investors? To this question, imperialists had a ready answer: imperialism, they said, brought the benefits of civilization to backward peoples. This argument found favor not only with the rich, who stood to profit by imperialism, but among Europeans of all classes. Leading churchmen, teachers, and writers championed the civilizing mission of imperialism as a duty which Christians should gladly undertake, and millions of ordinary people agreed. To them, imperialism was a kind of crusade in the name of Christianity, civilization, and country. This view came to be summed up in the phrase "the White Man's burden," from a famous poem by the ardently imperialistic English writer Rudyard Kipling:

> *Take up the White Man's burden—*
> *Send forth the best ye breed—*
> *Go bind your sons to exile*
> *To serve your captives' need;*
> *To wait in heavy harness*
> *On fluttered folk and wild—*
> *Your new-caught, sullen peoples,*
> *Half devil and half child.*

Among the imperialist powers, Great Britain came out the biggest winner when the First World War brought the international race for empires to a stop. By 1914, world maps showed a full quarter of the earth's land surface in red, meaning that it was British. Twenty billion dollars of British money, a quarter of the nation's wealth, was invested overseas.

India and the Indies
1856-1914

In 1856, Great Britain was at war with Russia in the Black Sea area and with the Chinese emperor in south China. Many British troops had been withdrawn from India to fight on these battlefronts. As a result, nine-tenths of the 200,000-man army guarding Great Britain's largest and richest possession, the subcontinent of India in south-central Asia, consisted of native soldiers called sepoys.

At the time, the British were putting a new type of rifle into service in the Indian Army. To load it, a rifleman had to insert each cartridge

AN INDIAN PAINTED ONE OF HIS BRITISH RULERS AS HE SAW HIM.

1055

THE BRITISH IMPRESSED THEIR INDIAN SUBJECTS WITH GREAT PROCESSIONS.

separately, and the cartridges were covered with grease. In January of 1857, rumors began to circulate among the sepoys in the Ganges Valley. The cartridge grease, it was whispered, came from animals. Moslems believed that it came from pigs, which their religion taught them to shun in any form, while Hindus believed it came from cows, which they held sacred. So sepoys of both religions refused to handle the new rifles.

THE SEPOY REVOLT

This refusal to bear arms was an act of mutiny which the British felt they could not leave unpunished. But punishment only made the sepoys desperate. On May 10, troops at the key post of Meerut massacred the British officers and their families. Other garrisons rebelled, and hordes of peasants and villagers, Moslem and Hindu, joined them. The uprising was supported by native princes, who were either fretting under British rule or feared that the British would soon take over their lands. By June, most of northeast India was in rebellion.

The Sepoy Revolt, as the rebellion was called, was the bloodiest event of Great Britain's long history in India. Hundreds of Englishmen were slain, some with their families, and countless thousands of Indians slaughtered in revenge by British troops and loyal sepoys. Cities were burned, looted, and laid waste. Not until 1859, when the last rebel leader was tracked down and killed, did the violence end.

This great upheaval marked a turning point in Anglo-Indian affairs, for it led to basic reforms in British rule. An outworn system of government was discarded and a more just and efficient system set up in its place. The old system, a patchwork of policies and customs, had grown up slowly over more than a century.

India had been known in the West since ancient times. After Vasco da Gama's famous voyage there in 1499, his fellow Portuguese set up trading posts where they bought Indian goods —spices, tea, silks, precious stones, and gorgeously wrought and woven stuffs—to bring back

India and the Indies

to Europe in their ships. In the sixteenth century, Dutch traders took over most of the trade, but in the seventeenth century they lost all but a small share of it to traders from Great Britain and France.

These two powers were often at war during the eighteenth century, and their forces in India battled over ports and territories. Slowly, the British defeated the French and drove them out. By the start of the nineteenth century, the British controlled about half of the vast peninsula, leaving their rivals only a few scraps of land on the coasts.

From London, the British government sent governors to India. But instead of ruling the country by themselves, the governors shared power with agents of the East India Company. For British India was not yet a British possession; it was a huge private holding of the trading company, operated for the benefit of its stockholders in Great Britain.

As time passed, however, the government became more deeply involved in Indian affairs. Its judges administered the laws, its fleets patrolled the surrounding ocean, and its Indian Army, made up mostly of native soldiers under British officers, kept order in the land. One by one, it took over tasks of administration from the company.

Still the British did not rule openly. They preferred to govern in the name of Indian rulers with great prestige but little power. Although the Mogul Empire, which had once dominated all India, had long since lost real power, the British pretended it was as strong as ever. They made yearly payments to Mogul overlords, descendants of the last real emperors, for the use of Mogul seals on official papers. As a rule,

THE SEPOY REVOLT WAS PUT DOWN AFTER A LONG AND BLOODY WAR. THE BRITISH DISARMED THIS NATIVE REGIMENT IN FRONT OF THE TAJ MAHAL.

1057

BRITISH AND FRENCH SOLDIERS BURNED DOWN THE SUMMER PALACE IN PEKING.

This made trading difficult. For generations the British East India Company had solved the problem of how to get Chinese tea by shipping the Chinese a drug called opium, made from the seeds of poppies grown in India. Opium could be either eaten or smoked. It put the user to sleep, eased his pain, or made him see visions. But it was habit-forming, and people who took it found that they could not stop.

In 1841, the Manchus tried to control the importing of the dangerous drug into their empire. The British immediately attacked China and forced the government to leave their trade alone. This brief conflict was the First Opium War.

Fifteen years later, the Chinese again tried to regulate the opium trade. This time, the British persuaded the French to invade China with them. In this war, the Second Opium War, the Europeans demanded more than the right to send as much opium as they liked into the country. They wanted to force the Chinese to receive their ambassadors and deal with their traders.

When the Chinese refused, the British and French soldiers marched into Peking, the Chinese capital, and set fire to the Emperor's Summer Palace. They looted the majestic old building of its treasures—vases, tapestries, porcelain, enam-

The Powers Carve Up China

els, jades, and wood-carvings. The soldiers brought so much loot home with them that Chinese art set a new fashion in Europe and America.

Both Opium Wars resulted in treaties, which in turn gave rise to treaties between China and other powers besides Great Britain and France. By the "treaty system," as it came to be called, China gave up many rights and some land to foreign powers. In return, the foreigners agreed to prop up the shaky Manchu government with their military and naval might.

In 1842, the Chinese handed over the port of Hong Kong to the British. They opened more than a dozen other coastal cities to foreign ships, including Shanghai and Canton. In these "treaty ports" foreigners lived in their own settlements, beyond the reach of Chinese laws, and even when they traveled in the empire they had to obey only the laws of their home countries. European and American gunboats patrolled the Yangtze River. The Chinese agreed not to charge duties on foreign goods greater than one-twentieth of their worth. Foreigners, not Chinese, collected the customs. Part of this money went to the foreign governments, and part to their feeble ally, the Manchu government.

But while they were supporting the Manchu emperors with money and arms, the foreign powers humiliated them by snatching slices of their territory. Patriotic Chinese burned with shame to see their country carved away at the edges. They hated both the foreigners for doing it and the Manchus for allowing it, but they were too weak to stop it.

In 1883, France seized Annam and combined it with its other possessions in Southeast Asia to make French Indo-China. Three years later the British took over Burma, on the eastern flank of India. Then, in 1894, a non-European power suddenly made its bid for a share of the loot. This power was Japan. It invaded Korea, and the following year forced China to give up Korea, the island of Formosa, and the Liaotung Peninsula in south Manchuria. Although the captured lands did not lie within the Chinese Empire, they had paid tribute to the emperor for centuries, and their loss was a blow to the Chinese.

The Russians, who had built the Pacific port of Vladivostok a generation before and were constructing the Trans-Siberian Railway connecting it with Europe, feared that Japan wanted to dominate their neighbor, Manchuria. Backed by the French and the Germans, they forced the Japanese to withdraw from the Liaotung Peninsula and its seaport, Port Arthur. The peninsula was returned to China.

But the European powers had no desire to strengthen China, and they were suspicious of Japan. In 1898, they acted together in an effort to get still more Chinese territory. They wrung long-term leases from the Manchu government, which, as usual, was willing to give up land and rights for hard cash.

In this way, Germany acquired Kiaochow Bay and trading rights on the Shantung Peninsula. Russia leased the Liaotung Peninsula and gained the right to build a railway from Port Arthur across Manchuria to link up with its Trans-Siberian line. France took Kwangchow and Great Britain Wei-hai-wei; the British also enlarged their "sphere of influence" in the Yangtze Valley. Even Italy demanded a piece of China, but the other powers blocked its demand. Of the countries trading with China, only the United States neither claimed nor received territory.

The American government, fearing that China's entire coast might soon be parceled out, announced that it favored what came to be called the Open Door Policy. It said that China should remain intact and independent, and that the powers with special rights in the country should keep the Chinese tariff at five per cent and allow businessmen of all nations to trade there. The British supported the Open Door Policy, partly to prevent China's land-hungry neighbors, Russia and Japan, from seizing Chinese territory.

THE BOXER REBELLION

But the Open Door Policy did nothing to soothe the outraged feelings of the Chinese. In 1899, a secret society broke out in rebellion against the foreigners. Its name, literally translated, was the Order of Literary Patriotic Harmonious Fists, which the foreigners jokingly turned into "Boxers." The Boxers tore up railway tracks, laid siege to the foreign quarters, and massacred foreigners and Chinese Christians. An international force, including Japanese and American soldiers, put them down after a brief, fierce struggle.

To make up for their losses, the victors fined

the Chinese government $330,000,000, and imposed even stricter controls than before. But the Boxer Rebellion had other and more important results. It made the Manchu officials try to adopt Western ways as fast as possible. It added to the national pride of many Chinese, and renewed their hope of forcing both the foreigners and the Manchus out of China. Revolutionary activity spread rapidly, especially in the south.

Gradually, a democratic thinker and man of action named Dr. Sun Yat-sen came to the fore as the leader of the rebels. In 1911, the rebels overthrew the Manchus and proclaimed China a republic, with Dr. Sun as its first president. In a short time, however, Sun resigned, believing that General Yuan Shih-kai could better unify the country.

But General Yuan did not really believe in democracy; he set up a military dictatorship and plotted to make himself emperor. When he died in 1916, the warlords in Peking scrambled for power. Dr. Sun became president of a rival southern republic with its capital in Canton. Because China was divided, it was still too weak to get rid of the hated "treaty system" and become a strong, democratic nation.

Japan Meets the West
1853-1905

The date was July 8, 1853; the place, Yedo, a sprawling collection of wooden houses overlooking an arm of the Pacific Ocean. Yedo, later known as Tokyo, was the chief city of the Japanese islands, off the east coast of Asia. It was larger than London or Paris, but since Japan had been out of touch with the rest of the world for centuries, few foreigners knew it. Yedo was also the residence of an official called the shogun, who theoretically governed the country in the name of the emperor. As they stared out at the bay that day, the people of Yedo could hardly believe what was happening before their eyes. In spite of a strong wind blowing seaward, four black ships were moving steadily toward them, trailing streamers of black smoke. Panic seized the onlookers, and they rushed to defend themselves.

The strange craft turned out to be warships from a distant land called the United States. They were commanded by an officer named Matthew Perry. But Perry had not come to attack Yedo; instead, he bore a friendly letter from the American president to the Japanese emperor. He asked the shogun's representatives to deliver it and sailed away, promising to come back.

The following February, Perry returned, this time with seven black ships. The officials who greeted him enjoyed the whiskey and other liq-

1062

JAPANESE OFFICIALS ASSEMBLED TO GREET PERRY AND HIS PARTY.

uors he gave them, and marveled at working models of a telegraph system and a steam locomotive. After a round of parties, talks began between the visitors and their hosts and on March 31, 1854, a treaty was signed between Japan and the United States.

Although this treaty opened only two small Japanese ports to American traders, it was of great importance, for it cleared the way for many other treaties between Japan and the Western powers. Soon, ships from several countries began calling at Yedo and other large seaports. Japan's long isolation was over, and within a few years its leaders had begun to transform it into a modern industrial state.

More than three centuries before, in 1542, Portuguese traders making their way north from India and China had come upon the Japanese islands. For almost a hundred years after that, European merchants and missionaries were active in Japan, but in 1640 the shogun forced them to sail away. Only a few Dutch merchants were allowed to stay, confined to the port of Nagasaki under strict control. These few Dutchmen were Japan's only link with the West, and through them, the Japanese learned a little of what was happening elsewhere. But the outside world knew practically nothing of what went on in the sealed-off island empire.

Under the Tokugawa shoguns, who ruled from

and Japanese dignitaries met in Portsmouth, New Hampshire, half-way around the world from where the fighting had taken place. By the Treaty of Portsmouth, Japan recovered Port Arthur and the Liaotung Peninsula. It gained a favored position in Manchuria, although Manchuria remained, in theory, subject to the emperor of China. Japan was recognized as the "protector" of Korea, and it received from Russia the southern half of the island of Sakhalin.

The Russo-Japanese War was the first war between great powers caused by competition for undeveloped lands. More important, it was the first war since ancient times in which non-whites had defeated whites. As news of it spread, the yellow- and brown-skinned peoples of Asia took heart. Japan's defeat of Russia showed that the Europeans were not gods. In China, the East Indies, India and other countries, people began to ask themselves a significant question: if the Japanese could force out a Western power, why can't we?

THE JAPANESE VICTORY OVER THE RUSSIANS IN TSUSHIMA STRAIT WAS THE FIRST TIME AN ASIAN NATION HAD DEFEATED A MODERN EUROPEAN POWER.

Parceling Out a Continent
1841-1910

Africa, the second largest continent in the world, extends south from the Mediterranean Sea four thousand miles. Along its north coast is a strip of land known to Europeans since ancient times. South of this strip lie mountains and deserts. The Sahara, an empty "sea" of sand and rock, crosses the continent in a belt several hundreds of miles wide; it is hot and dry, vast and rugged. Europeans knew very little about the lands beyond it. Almost all they knew of Africa were the coasts, which they could reach by sea. As late as the time of the American Civil War and the unification of Italy and Germany, Africa was still largely unknown—the "Dark Continent."

The people of North Africa were white—descendants of the early inhabitants and of Arabs who had conquered them for Islam. South of the Sahara lay "Black Africa," a land of Negroes. The Negroes were divided into thousands of tribes, but had no organized states. They spoke hundreds of languages, but had no writing. They lived by hunting, raising cattle, and simple farming, and worshiped tribal gods. All of Black Africa was Negro except for a few places on the Indian Ocean where Arab traders had settled, and the southernmost part of the continent, where some European families had settled.

STANLEY AND LIVINGSTON

In the sixteenth century, Portuguese and Spanish ships had begun to stop at points on the Atlantic shore of Africa to trade. Later, traders came from other European countries. The names they gave to stretches of shoreland—the Gold Coast, the Ivory Coast, the Slave Coast—show what they came for. But the Europeans found that the sultry coastland was ridden with disease. So many of them died there that West Africa came to be known as "the white man's graveyard." After a few disastrous tries, they gave up the idea of establishing white settlements.

When the Europeans sailed farther south, however, they found the air fresher and cooler and the coastland free of diseases. The southern end of the continent was particulary inviting. Much of it was open grassland instead of jungle, it was neither too hot nor too cold, and it contained few people. In the seventeenth century, Dutch families began to settle at the southern most tip of Africa. Farther north, where the natives were more numerous, the Portuguese set up colonies on both coasts—Angola on the Atlantic and Mozambique on the Indian Ocean. But for another two hundred years the interior of the continent remained a mystery.

Missionaries, explorers, and men of action opened up Africa to Europe. In 1841, David Livingstone, a Scottish doctor, went to southeast Africa as a medical missionary. For many years he traveled through a huge area which appeared on maps as a blank, preaching Christianity in African languages and healing the sick. He explored the Zambesi River and discovered, among other natural wonders, the world's most majestic waterfall, Victoria Falls. Safe among his African friends, he only wanted to go on with his work undisturbed.

Then a rumor that Livingstone was lost reached Europe and America. As a stunt to make news, the New York *Herald* sent Henry M. Stanley to Africa to find Livingstone. When he did find Livingstone at a village calle Ujiji, he is supposed to have said: "Doctor Livingstone, I presume." Soon after their meeting, Livingstone died, lamented by the natives.

Stanley was a very different kind of man from Livingstone. To him, Africa was a land that offered unlimited opportunities for making money. Brimming with ideas, he went to Europe to look for backers, and in 1878 he found one in King Leopold of Belgium.

The king was already thinking of developing the basin of the Congo River, in Central Africa, and Stanley's talk stirred him to action. With a few financiers, the two men founded the International Congo Association. The association had no connection with the Belgian government. It was a private enterprise, set up to get whatever could be gotten out of the Congo for the benefit of King Leopold and his friends.

Returning to the Congo in 1882, Stanley traveled up the great river and through the surrounding jungle. Wherever he went, he persuaded the chief of the local tribe to put his mark on a piece of paper, in return for a few trinkets or bolts of cloth. The paper gave the association the right to use the tribe's land. Since the chief could not read and had never heard of private property, he of course did not understand what he was agreeing to. But his crude mark and his acceptance of a blue-and-gold association flag were enough. Within a year, Stanley made treaties with more than five hundred chiefs.

Meanwhile, other explorers were doing the same thing elsewhere in Africa for their governments. North of the Congo, a Frenchman named Brazza handed out French flags in every village he visited, until he claimed a territory larger than France. From Zanzibar, on the east coast of Africa, Karl Peters, a German, worked his way inland, making treaties. Farther south, the Portuguese took steps to unite Angola and Mozambique in one large colony that stretched coast to coast. Throughout Black Africa there were still no definite boundaries, and no one could be sure where one country's claim ended and another's began.

In 1885 the German chancellor, Bismarck, invited the imperial powers to send emissaries to Berlin to clear up the confusion. The Berlin conference recognized King Leopold's holdings as the Congo Free State, and set boundaries which gave it an area almost as large as the United States east of the Mississippi River. The powers agreed that everyone should be allowed to do business in the Congo, that no tariff should be levied on goods arriving there, and that the slave trade should be stamped out. As the person who owned and governed the country, Leopold was expected to carry out the agreements.

But the conference failed to set up effective safeguards, and Leopold did as he pleased. His greed for profits led to horrifying cruelties. Europe and America wanted rubber, more and more of it, and the Congo was then one of the few places in the world that produced raw rubber. The primitive Congolese, weakened by disease and the damp heat of their lowland equatorial home, could only be made to tap enough rubber trees by force. White overseers, under orders to produce a certain amount of rubber, had their workers whipped and beaten without mercy. A native who shirked or ran way or was caught stealing might have a leg or an arm cut off, and tens of thousands of Congolese died in misery.

Leopold's personal income from the rubber plantations was huge; it enabled him to live in great luxury in Brussels. But even inhuman measures failed to make the Congo profitable; the enterprise as a whole lost money. To pay off its debts, the king borrowed a large sum from the Belgian government. He agreed that Belgium should inherit the Congo if he did not pay the money back. When he died in 1908, the Congo Free State became the Belgian Congo, and Belgian administrators did away with the worst abuses of Leopold's rule.

The Berlin conference of 1885 had also laid down rules for all the powers seeking land in Africa. Colonies and trading posts on the coast gave a power the right to territory inland. But to make its claim stick, the power had to station troops and administrators there after informing

STANLEY'S MEETING WITH LIVINGSTON BECAME FAMOUS THROUGHOUT THE WORLD.

the other powers of its plans. This led to a wild scramble to occupy Africa. In fifteen years the entire continent was parcelled out, except for Ethiopia and little Liberia on the west coast, founded in 1822 as a homeland for freed American slaves.

Between 1885 and 1900 the Portuguese greatly enlarged Angola and Mozambique. Italy took over two barren tracts, Italian Somaliland and Eritrea. From them, troops marched inland to win the richer prize of Ethiopia. But in 1896, at Adowa, 80,000 Ethiopians slaughtered 20,000 Italians, the first time Africans had successfully defended themselves against whites. Not for forty years would Italy or any other power invade Ethiopia again.

MEETING AT FASHODA

The chief contenders for African territory were Great Britain, France, and Germany. Each was jealous and suspicious of the others, and preferred to leave territories in the hands of minor powers rather than see them taken over by one of its rivals. For this reason, Portugal, Italy, Spain, and the Congo Free State were able to seize large areas for themselves, as, meanwhile, the struggle among the three great powers grew even more intense.

Germany, the last of the three to enter the competition, established colonies in German East Africa, the Cameroons and Togo on the west coast, and German Southwest Africa. France, too, wanted a trans-African empire. It already controlled most of West Africa—whose coast, thanks to modern medicine, was no longer "the white man's graveyard"—and tiny French Somaliland, on the Gulf of Aden. The French dreamed of creating a French belt across North Africa from the Atlantic to the Red Sea, and to do this they had to have the region south of Egypt, known as the Sudan.

But Great Britain also had its dream, which was summed up in the slogan: "Africa British from the Cape to Cairo." The British plan called for a belt of colonies running north and south; this conflicted with the French plan for a belt of colonies running east and west. And the British were in a good position to carry out their plan. From the Cape of Good Hope, they pushed north into Rhodesia. Kenya and Uganda,

in East Africa, were already theirs, and Egypt had been under their "protection" since 1882. Egypt had long claimed the Sudan, out of which the Nile River flowed, and the British had backed its claim. The first British attempt to subdue the wild Sudanese tribesmen had failed. But in 1898 a force under General Kitchener pushed south up the Nile, took Omdurman, and continued upstream.

At the same time, a small French force led by a Captain Marchand was making its way east from Lake Chad. Its orders were to hoist the French flag on the upper Nile and claim the Sudan for France. Suddenly, at a place called Fashoda, the French came face to face with the larger British force. The meeting was one of the most awkward moments of modern history. Neither Kitchener nor Marchand knew what to do; each sent word to his government and waited for orders.

The dramatic meeting at Fashoda became a showdown between Great Britain and France, a test of the ability of each government to carry out its imperial ambitions. At first, both refused to budge. Then the British threatened to fight. The French, afraid that the Germans might attack them in Europe, decided at last not to take the risk and recalled Captain Marchand from Fashoda.

THE BOER WAR

No sooner had the British won this victory than they became entangled in another struggle at the other end of Africa from the Sudan. This struggle was the Boer War. The Boers were descendants of the Dutchmen who had settled the Cape of Good Hope in the seventeenth century; their name came from the Dutch word for farmer. After 1815, when Great Britain acquired the Cape, the Boers had made a "great trek" inland to escape British rule. There they had eventually set up two small independent republics, the Transvaal and the Orange Free State. A simple, old-fashioned people, the Boers saw nothing wrong in keeping Negro slaves and disliked all "Uitlanders," or outlanders, who sought to invade their privacy.

In 1890 Cecil Rhodes became prime minister of Britain's Cape Colony. The world's foremost empire-builder in an age of empire building,

THE BOERS USED GUERRILLA TACTICS IN THEIR WAR AGAINST THE BRITISH.

he forcefully pushed the "Cape to Cairo" plan. But the two Boer republics stood in his way. When gold and diamonds were discovered in the Transvaal, the British poured in, but the Boers refused to let the Uitlanders dig mines. In 1895, Rhodes sent armed men under a friend named Dr. Jameson into the Transvaal, hoping to start a revolution which would overthrow the government.

The Jameson Raid failed, but many people in Europe were shocked to see the British bullying their small neighbor. The Germans, particularly, were indignant. Their emperor sent a message to Paul Kruger, the president of the Transvaal, congratulating him for driving off the invaders "without having to call for the support of friendly powers." By "friendly powers" the emperor meant Germany.

Three years later the British went to war with the Boer republics. The Boers were hardy frontiersmen who knew the countryside well, and, accustomed to hunting from childhood, they were skilled riflemen. At first the British troops were no match for their enemies. In time, however, they learned something of the countryside and adopted the Boer's methods of guerrilla warfare. They began to push the Boers back, and at last, in 1901, the Boer republics surrendered.

On being taken into the British Empire, the Transvaal and the Orange Free State kept their governments and laws. In 1910, they joined Natal and Cape Colony, whose white inhabitants were mostly British, in the Union of South Africa. The Union was a self-governing territory like Canada, that owed allegiance to the British Crown.

Rivalries in the Middle East

1856-1912

THE MIDDLE EAST, where Europe, Asia and Africa meet, had long been known as one of the great crossroads of the world. Most of its people were Moslems, but among them were many Christians and Jews. They spoke languages as different as Arabic and Latin, Slavic and Turkish. They had little in common except that they were all subjects of the Ottoman sultan in Constantinople.

The Ottoman Empire—so called after its early founder, Othman—was the last of several empires to rule over a large part of Islam. Unlike the earlier empires, it was dominated not by Arabs, but by Turks. Centuries before, the Turks had fought their way west from Central Asia and founded a new homeland in the West Asian peninsula of Turkey. From there, they had pushed outward, conquering lands and peoples. In 1699, however, they had lost Hungary to the Austrians. After that, while the nations of western Europe grew stronger, the Ottoman Empire became weaker.

Throughout the eighteenth, nineteenth, and early twentieth centuries, the Ottoman sultans had to combat enemies both within and without their empire. Their foreign enemies were the European powers, which snatched up their outlying lands. Their enemies at home were the subject peoples, especially in the Balkan Peninsula of southeast Europe, who demanded their freedom. Unrest was chronic, and the Ottoman Empire, which was usually called simply Turkey, came to be known as "the sick man of Europe."

By the 1850's, Turkey had lost lands north of the Black Sea to Russia, and Algeria, in North Africa, to France. Of its former Balkan holdings, Greece was independent and both Serbia and Rumania had some freedom. A native Arab dynasty ruled much of Arabia. In Egypt, a former Turkish governor had set himself up as hereditary khedive, or viceroy. But the Ottoman holdings were still huge, reaching from Tunisia to the shores of the Red Sea and Persian Gulf.

In the Crimean War of 1854-56, the Turks were rescued from the attacking Russians by the British and French. The war showed them how far behind the Europeans they were in science, technology, and practically everything else that counted in the modern world. They saw they must either strengthen their empire or watch it fall to pieces. In 1856, the sultan announced sweeping changes. Moslems as well as Christians and Jews were now required to pay taxes. Torture was abolished, and strict punishments set for dishonest officials.

ABDUL THE DAMNED

For twenty years the reformers strove to bring the creaky old empire up to date. Newspapers were printed and liberal Western ideas circulated. Schools and colleges were founded, including an American school, Roberts College. The government borrowed money abroad and a railroad was built between the Black Sea and the Danube River. And the subject peoples were given a greater say in their affairs.

But the reformers had enemies in high places. The powerful religious leaders, unwilling to give up their authority over their followers, resisted them strongly. Reforms were blocked by ordinary men, too. The Balkan peoples, for instance, no longer thought of themselves as Christian subjects of a Moslem ruler, but as Bulgars, Greeks, Rumanians, Serbs, or Armenians. They cared nothing about reforming the Ottoman Empire; they wanted to get out of it, and they were willing to fight for their freedom.

In 1876, a new sultan, Abdul Hamid, came to power. He issued a constitution which promised his subjects personal liberty, freedom of religion, education, and the press, and an elected government. But the next year he showed his true colors. The first parliament in Turkish history had hardly met when he sent its members home and tore up the constitution.

Abdul Hamid crushed the reformers' hope of a Turkish revival. He lived, as one historian wrote, "like a terrified animal, fighting back blindly and fiercely against forces that he could not understand." His fear of all change infected his entire government. When a shipment of dynamos arrived in Constantinople the Turkish customs officers learned that the dynamos made several hundred revolutions a minute. Fearful even of the word "revolution," they refused to let the dynamos into the country. Chemistry books for the American college were destroyed out of fear that the chemical symbols on their pages were coded messages to agitators plotting against the government.

Panicked by the slightest move to modernize Turkey, the sultan put all the reformers he could into prison, where they were tortured and killed. The reformers fought back by assassinating his officials. Thousands of persons fled into exile, especially to Paris, where they plotted to overthrow "Abdul the Damned." The sultan was frightened, too, of nationalist agitation among his non-Turkish subjects. On his orders, Turkish troops slaughtered uncounted tens of thousands of peasants—Bulgarians, Armenians, and others. The massacres horrified the people of western Europe, who demanded that their leaders do something about it. But while the West European governments deplored the bloodshed, they had no intention of supporting the aim of the Turkish reformers. They all had interests in the Middle East and wanted to keep "the sick man of Europe" from recovering.

JINGOISM

Soon after the Suez Canal was opened in 1869, the British, who used it more than any other nation, began to think of it as their "lifeline of empire." In 1875 the British Prime Minister, Benjamin Disraeli, learned that the Khedive of Egypt was almost bankrupt. He immediately bought the Khedive's shares in the Suez Canal, amounting to almost half the total stock, and Great Britain became the chief owner of the canal.

But the canal was on Ottoman territory, and the Turks were again being threatened by the Russians. For generations, the Russians had dreamed of taking over the Bosphorus and the Dardanelles, the straits which led into and out of the Sea of Marmora. The straits would give Russia an outlet to the Mediterranean Sea. In claiming the Turkish territory, the tsar's government used the docrine called Pan-Slavism as an excuse.

Pan-Slavism was the idea that all peoples of Slavic birth must stand together. The Russians offered to help their fellow Slavs in the Balkans get rid of their Turkish masters, and to protect them thereafter. Many Bulgars, Serbs, and other Balkan Slavs feared that Russian "protection" would really mean Russian rule, but even so, they welcomed the Russian offer.

In 1877, Russia declared war on the Ottoman Empire. Its armies overran the Balkans, reached Constantinople, and forced the Turks to sign a treaty. The Treaty of San Stefano, as it was called, granted independence to Rumania and Serbia and some self-rule to a new state, Bulgaria. Alarmed by Russia's success, the British people clamored for war against Russia, and sang:

> *We don't want to fight,*
> *but by jingo, if we do,*
> *We've got the men,*
> *we've got the ships,*
> *we've got the money, too.*

From this popular song came a new word in the English language—"jingoism," meaning a warlike attitude toward a foreign nation.

Everyone knew that an Anglo-Russian war could easily become a European war. To prevent this, the German chancellor, Bismarck, summoned the powers of Europe to Berlin. To get them to agree on a settlement, it seemed necessary to give them something—and the gifts turned out to be parts of the Ottoman Empire. The Congress of Berlin kept peace in Europe at the expense of Turkey.

Russia was persuaded to give up the Treaty of San Stefano, but it kept its conquests on the south side of the Caucasus Mountains and won independence for the Serbs and Rumanians. Montenegro was also recognized as independent. Bulgaria was left in the Ottoman Empire, but divided into zones with more or less self-government. Austria-Hungary was allowed to occupy Bosnia, but not to annex it. Great Britain took over the large island of Cyprus, near Suez. France gained Tunisia, on the eastern flank of Algeria. Italy was put off with a vague hint that it might some day be allowed to occupy little Albania —for, as Bismarck privately complained, "the Italians have such a large appetite and such poor teeth." Germany took nothing. Bismarck boasted that he was an "honest broker," with no interest except peace.

Rivalries in the Middle East

"THE BIG THING."
OLD MOTHER SEWARD. "I'll rub some of this on his sore spot, it may soothe him a little."

SECRETARY SEWARD WAS RIDICULED FOR HIS PURCHASE OF ALASKA FROM RUSSIA.

The Treaty of Berlin did prevent war, but it left many problems unsolved. Neither the Russian Pan-Slavs nor the Balkan nationalists were satisfied with it. And both Abdul Hamid and the reformers who opposed him were furious over the further loss of Turkish territory.

In 1882, rioting broke out in the Egyptian port of Alexandria against the unpopular khedive and his British and French backers. British warships bombarded the city, and British troops landed, put down the riot, and took the khedive into their protection. Egypt was important to Great Britain, not only because of Suez, but also because it furnished much of the raw cotton used by British textile factories. The British set up a protectorate over the country, and they stayed on, to the annoyance of the French, who consoled themselves by pushing west from Algeria into Morocco. This move displeased both the British and the Germans. Thus rivalry over the spoils of the Ottoman Empire caused bad feeling among the powers.

In 1908, Turkish reformers finally seized power from the aged Abdul Hamid. They hurriedly pushed through reforms, but they acted too late to hold on to what was left of the empire. By this time, Bulgaria had declared its independence, and Austria-Hungary had annexed Bosnia. In 1911 and 1912, Italy seized the Dodecanese Islands and Libya, in North Africa. And in two Balkan Wars, in 1912 and 1913, Turkey lost almost all of its territory in Europe to Bulgaria, Serbia and Greece, and to Albania, which became independent in 1912.

Meanwhile, to the growing concern of Great Britain, France, and Russia, Germany had gained more and more influence in Turkey. German engineers had planned and partly built—with German money—a great railway to run from Berlin all the way to Bagdad. This railway, when completed, would give Germany access to important Middle Eastern resources, including oil. The British were particularly unhappy about this project, which they saw as a threat to their empire in India.

The United States and Destiny
1848-1914

THE UNITED STATES entered the race for colonies last of all the powers, at the end of the nineteenth century. Long before then, however, Americans were accustomed to taking over territory; they had, in fact, built their country westward from the Atlantic by settling lands they had bought or seized. And in the Mexican War of 1845-48, they had taken a huge tract of land from Mexico by force.

Many Americans, including Abraham Lincoln, believed that the Mexican War was simply an invasion of a weak country by its powerful, land-hungry neighbor. But others maintained that the move was justified by the country's needs. They

1074

pointed out that the United States was the largest, richest, and most advanced nation in North America, with the fastest-growing population. For these reasons, they said, it was entitled to take the land it needed. This was the doctrine of "manifest destiny." Its supporters believed that before long the United States was bound to dominate the continent, if not the entire hemisphere.

With the land it had gained in the Mexican War, the United States spanned North America from ocean to ocean. Talk of manifest destiny died down, for most Americans felt that the country had reached its limits. When Secretary of State William Seward bought Alaska from Russia in 1867, he was widely criticized. People said Alaska was nothing but a frozen wasteland, and called it "Seward's Icebox." And for a time they were too busy building up their own country to bother much about other lands.

By the 1890's, however, the United States was a great industrial power, and had trade links with several other parts of the world besides its old trading partners in Europe. Millions of American dollars were invested in neighboring Latin American republics, and American trade with the Far East, especially China, was growing. Americans began to look beyond their borders —south to Central and South America, and west across the Pacific. Like the western Europeans before them, they felt that they must have an empire.

From pulpits and platforms, in the halls of Congress and the editorial columns of newspapers, arguments long familiar to Europeans were put forward. Imperialism was the mark of a modern industrial state. The United States must expand overseas, not only for the sake of its commercial and financial interests, but also to show the world that it was indeed a great and powerful nation. America, too, wanted its "place in the sun," and national pride demanded it.

Listening to such talk, many Americans felt uneasy. They reminded their countrymen that the United States had come into being by freeing itself from the British Empire; was it right for such a nation to impose its rule on others? But such objections were swept aside, and in 1898, for the first time in its history, the United States took over territory outside North America.

One such territory was the Hawaiian Islands, formerly the Sandwich Islands, in the mid-Pacific, four thousand miles from California. They had long been ruled by native kings, but in the nineteenth century, as whaling and trade developed in the Pacific, they came under the domination of, first, Britain, and then the United States. After about 1875, real control was in the hands of American planters, who had large sugar and pineapple plantations on the islands, and the American shipowners who transported their produce to the mainland.

In 1891, Queen Liliuokalani came to the throne. A woman of great spirit and energy, Liliuokalani wanted to rid the land of foreign influence and restore the old Hawaiian ways. But the American planters would not stand for this; they overthrew the queen, set up a republic, and invited the United States to take over.

REMEMBER THE MAINE!

For several years the American government did nothing, not wishing to seem to approve of the planters' strong-arm methods. But in 1894 Japan showed its strength by attacking China, and in the next few years other powers snatched more territory from the Manchu Empire. Finally, in 1898, the United States itself became a Pacific power by taking the Philippine Islands from Spain. In the same year, it "accepted its destiny" and annexed the Republic of Hawaii.

The old, half-forgotten doctrine of "manifest destiny" was thus revived in a new form. Fifty years before, the doctrine had been used to justify taking over sparsely settled neighboring territory for one purpose—settlement. Now, it had been stretched to cover lands cut off from the United States by sea, lands which had large native populations and were sometimes unsuitable for settlement by anyone else. The doctrine had come to mean that the country had both a right and a duty to take over such lands—to keep them out of the hands of unfriendly powers, to make use of their natural resources, to educate and uplift their peoples. In its new form, manifest destiny had much in common with Kipling's appeal to "take up the White Man's burden."

Of Spain's once-vast empire in the Americas, all that remained was the large Caribbean island of Cuba and its smaller neighbor, Puerto Rico. For generations, the people of Cuba had periodically rebelled against their Spanish masters. Be-

THE SINKING OF THE *MAINE* IN HAVANA HARBOR SET OFF THE WAR WITH SPAIN.

cause Cuba lay only ninety miles from Florida and American businessmen had large sugar plantations there, many Americans knew of the islanders' struggle and sided with them in their fight for *Cuba Libre,* a free Cuba.

When a Spanish general named Weyler arrived in Cuba in 1897 to put down the latest uprising, American newspapers rushed reporters and artists to the island. Day after day they published illustrated stories, under bold, black headlines, telling of horrible cruelties inflicted on the Cubans by the soldiers of "Butcher" Weyler. Throughout the country, sympathy for the Cubans and indignation against the Spaniards mounted.

Then, in February of 1898, the United States battleship *Maine,* on a visit to the Cuban capital, Havana, suddenly blew up in an explosion that killed more than 250 officers and men. The cause of the disaster was never discovered, but millions of Americans immediately blamed the Spanish authorities. Newspapers clamored for war. In the streets of the cities, people waved American flags and chanted a new slogan:

> Remember the Maine!
> To hell with Spain!

While American and Spanish diplomats tried to preserve peace, war fever gripped both countries. In Congress, the war party grew louder and more numerous. At last, in April, President William McKinley gave in and signed the order which sent the country to war.

The United States easily defeated Spain. It quickly conquered Cuba, Puerto Rico, and then —to the surprise of most Americans, who had never heard of it—a large group of islands called the Philippines, on the other side of the globe. By August, the fighting was over. Puerto Rico and the Philippines were annexed outright, together with the small South Pacific island of Guam. Cuba became an independent republic. But since the United States kept the right to watch over Cuba's relations with foreign countries and send troops there to restore order in matters of "life, property, individual liberty and Cuban independence," it was really an American protectorate.

And so, in the single year 1898, a country which had itself been made up of colonies only a few generations before acquired a considerable overseas empire. But before the Americans could learn much about their richest new possession, the Philippines, a serious revolt broke out there. The Filipinos had expected to become free at last, after four centuries of Spanish rule; that was why they had helped the Americans. When they found that they would now be under the rule of the United States, they took to the hills and began to raid American camps from jungle hideouts. The American soldiers found the task of combatting them in the unfamiliar tropical countryside maddeningly slow and difficult After much bloodshed, the rebels were finally put down when their leader, "General" Aguinaldo, was captured in 1902. Americans were learning that imperialism was not all glory.

Even so, their new president, Theodore Roosevelt, urged them on. In the war with Spain, Roosevelt had fought in Cuba, and, as a mere assistant secretary of the Navy, he had ordered Admiral George Dewey to take Manila, the Philippine capital. As President from 1901 to 1909, he vigorously and enthusiastically promoted imperialism. Once, referring to a West African proverb, he declared that nations, like people, should "walk softly and carry a big stick."

1077

AMERICAN ENGINEERS TOOK TEN YEARS TO CONSTRUCT THE PANAMA CANAL.

In 1904, Roosevelt warned the Latin American countries that "behavior which results in a general loosening of the ties of civilization may require intervention by some civilized nation." The Monroe Doctrine, a keystone of American foreign policy since 1823, barred the European powers from meddling in the western hemisphere. Therefore, he concluded, the United States might be forced "to the exercise of an international police power."

The next year, the island republic of Santo Domingo became bankrupt, to the alarm of its creditors in Europe. Before the European powers could take action, Roosevelt sent financial experts to Santo Domingo. They straightened out the country's tangled finances and collected half of its customs in order to pay back the Europeans. In this way, he put into effect what came to be called the Roosevelt Corollary (or addition) to the Monroe Doctrine.

The Roosevelt Corollary supposedly gave the United States the right to intervene in the Western Hemisphere wherever, whenever, and however it chose. From the first, proud Latin Americans bitterly resented this doctrine, particularly because of its insulting suggestion that the United States was "civilized" while they were not. The Cubans were just as resentful of the provisions in their constitution which gave the United States

ama; it gave up the attempt when it ran out of money. The company wanted to be paid for its rights and its leftover equipment. One of its agents came to Washington, where he talked to government leaders, including Roosevelt. Partly because of his efforts, Congress voted to build the canal in Panama rather than Nicaragua. But the Colombian government still said that the price offered for the land was too low.

At this, Roosevelt lost patience. He schemed with agents of the French canal company and other men to bring about a revolution in Panama. On the appointed day, a tiny band of hired soldiers and Panamanians seized the isthmus. American warships, conveniently offshore, prevented Colombian troops from landing. The rebels proclaimed the independent republic of Panama. In the record time of two days, the United States recognized the new republic and received its ambassador—the French canal company's agent.

A treaty was quickly drawn up and signed, granting Panama ten million dollars and $250,000 a year for a strip of land ten miles wide across the isthmus. Digging began, and the Panama Canal was finally opened to interocean traffic in 1914.

After the Canal Zone episode, the United States gave up imperialistic adventures. There followed, instead, a long period of "dollar diplomacy," when the government at times sent soldiers and Marines into several foreign countries to protect its citizens' investments. "Dollar diplomacy" and the Roosevelt Corollary showed the difference between the European and American brands of imperialism. European powers frankly took over countries where they had commercial interests and governed them as colonies. The

the right to intervene in their affairs. These provisions were called, after the American lawmaker who framed them, the Platt Amendment. For more than a generation, the Roosevelt Corollary and the Platt Amendment were to sow bad feeling for the United States in the lands to the south.

Under Roosevelt, the United States acquired a strip of land across the Isthmus of Panama, the narrow waist of the Americas, and at last began to build the canal between the Atlantic and the Pacific Oceans. As usual, the energetic and impulsive President personally took part in the proceedings.

Until 1904, Panama was only a small and poor province of Colombia, at the northwest corner of South America. The United States, eager to start digging the canal, offered Colombia ten million dollars for a site. But Colombia held out for more. Congressmen and other government leaders then proposed that the canal be built across Nicaragua instead, but Roosevelt was determined to use the shorter, cheaper route across the isthmus.

A French company, originally headed by the creator of the Suez Canal, Ferdinand de Lesseps, had long before started to build a canal in Pan-

THE CANAL RUNS THROUGH THREE SETS OF LOCKS AND A HUGE MAN-MADE LAKE.

United States, by contrast, preferred to leave such countries independent, even though the financial power of American bankers and businessmen gave it enormous influence over them.

While many Latin Americans disliked this American influence, they were at least spared the indignity of direct American rule. And the time would come when the United States would repudiate the Platt Amendment and drop the offensive Roosevelt Corollary. "Dollar diplomacy" would be replaced by the "good neighbor policy," putting the Latin American countries on a more equal footing with the "Yankee Colossus."

Storm Clouds Over Europe
1882-1907

As the year 1899 drew to a close, Europeans and Americans began to wonder when, exactly, the nineteenth century would end and the twentieth century begin. Most people thought that this would take place at midnight of December 31, 1899. But historians disagreed. They pointed out that the first hundred years after the birth of Christ had ended with the final seconds of the year 100. Therefore, they said, the twentieth century would not begin until January 1, 1901.

As they toasted the new century that New Year's Day most people in Europe and America were satisfied and hopeful. Life was better for them than it had been for their fathers and grandfathers, and they were certain that it would be better still for their sons and grandsons. They believed in human progress, and looking back over the century just past, they could find good reasons for this belief.

There had been no widespread fighting in Europe since the end of the Napoleonic Wars in 1815. The last war between European powers, the Franco-Prussian War, had taken place in 1870. Since then, thirty years of peace had brought tremendous benefits to the advanced countries of Europe. The growth of industry and trade had steadily enriched these countries and raised their living standards. With the spread of education, millions of people had learned to read and write. Democratic ideas were advancing everywhere; by now, most European countries had law-making assemblies with elected members, and more people had the right to vote than ever before. And, as the powers had acquired territories on other continents, European ideas, beliefs, and methods had come to dominate the entire world.

Europeans were proud of their civilization, and confident of the future. True, they had problems at home and abroad, but they were sure that their parliaments and statesmen would find ways to solve them and keep the peace. Then, in 1914, Europe was plunged into war. By the time the war was over, four years later, much of the rest of the world had been drawn into it, including the United States; millions of men had died; and a way of life built up over half a century had been destroyed.

World War I marked the real end of the nineteenth century, for it changed the world and few things would ever be the same again. Europeans would remember the years before 1914 as a far happier time—a time of peace and order and security.

THE TRIPLE ALLIANCE

Why then did Europe go to war? There were several reasons, some clear enough at the time, and many not so clear. But all the reasons could be traced back to rivalry among the powers.

Before the war, the strongest nations in Europe were Great Britain, France, and Germany. The other industrial countries—Belgium, Holland, and Sweden—were too small to count in the balance of power, as were Denmark and Switzerland. Spain and Portugal had long ceased to play active roles in Europe. Italy, partly industrialized, yearned to be accepted as a power of the first rank, but could not back up its claims with real strength. The remaining powers were Austria-Hungary and Russia.

Austria-Hungary took up an impressive space on the map and had a large population. It was not a true nation, however, but a curious mixture of nations unlike any other. With an emperor of the Hapsburg family at their head, the Austrians and the Hungarians ruled as partners over a collection of subject peoples. Like the minority groups in the neighboring Ottoman Empire, these peoples wanted their freedom. And since most of them were Slavs, they were greatly attracted to the doctrine of Pan-Slavism.

Pan-Slavism came, of course, from Russia. Russia was far the largest of the powers, stretching across Asia all the way to the Pacific. But it was also the least industrialized, the least democratic, and the least advanced. Its ambitions in the Balkans kept it constantly at odds with Austria-Hungary.

From the moment it was proclaimed in 1871, the German Empire was the mightiest military power in Europe. But the German chancellor, Count Bismarck, feared that the other powers might tear the empire to pieces if they felt that it threatened their safety. And so he sought their friendship and tried to keep on good terms with them. In 1879, Germany formed an alliance with Austria-Hungary. Italy joined it three years later, forming what was known as the Triple Alliance. The three nations agreed that if one of them found itself at war with two or more powers, the other two members of the alliance would go to its aid.

To Bismarck, colonies were nothing but an expensive nuisance. He believed that the important thing was to build up Germany itself, especially its industry, and make it safe from attack. But Kaiser Wilhelm II, who became emperor of Germany in 1888, had different ideas. Two years after he came to the throne, he dismissed Bismarck and replaced him with a man who would carry out his wishes. After that, although Germany had an elected Parliament called the Reichstag, the kaiser ruled the empire himself, through officials of his choosing. Germany began actively to challenge the other powers, especially Great Britain and France, in three fields of competition—the colonies, the Balkans, and the high seas.

The contrast between Germany under Bismarck and Germany under Kaiser Wilhelm was summed up in the contrast between the two men. Bismarck, who had been nicknamed the Iron Chancellor because of his firm control over his country, was stout and paunchy, and had a white walrus moustache. He looked like many people's idea of a German grandfather—a man who was solemn, stern, and devoted to duty, who valued

KAISER WILHELM II OF GERMANY

order and discipline and at the same time enjoyed quantities of food and drink. While he was chancellor, he seemed typical of all Germans.

Kaiser Wilhelm was altogether different. He was lean, tense, with a black moustache that jutted upward in spikes from under a sharp nose. Having been brought up in the military tradition of the Prussian aristocracy, he held himself stiffly erect; he probably stood all the straighter to make up for the fact that his left arm had been withered from birth and hung useless at his side. He seldom wore anything but a military uniform. His bristling moustache, stiff posture, and uniform became known throughout the world when foreign cartoonists used him as a convenient symbol of a warlike Germany.

Bismarck had been the cleverest diplomat of his time. In spite of the Triple Alliance and Russia's rivalry in the Balkans with Austria-Hungary, he persuaded the Russians to renew a pact of mutual assistance he had made with them. But after he was removed from the post of chancellor the agreement was not renewed again. The French, worried by the Triple Alliance, took advantage of this opportunity and in 1894 formed an alliance with the Russians. It was called the Dual Alliance.

"FRIENDLY UNDERSTANDING"

The continental powers were now divided, with Germany, Austria-Hungary, and Italy on one side and France and Russia on the other. For a time, it looked as though the split between the two sides might be healed. In 1895, Germany helped France and Russia force the Japanese out of Manchuria. During the Fashoda Crisis and the Boer War, all five powers united against the British. Then Britain entered the competition for power, and the split instead of healing became wider.

For many years, the British had gone their own way, relying on their navy, the world's largest and strongest, to protect them at home and throughout their empire. But the violence of the anti-British feeling stirred up in Europe by the Fashoda Crisis and the Boer War gave them a shock. They suddenly felt alone and in need of friends. Their relations with France and Russia were very bad; perhaps Germany was their logical ally. Some Englishmen thought so, but others recalled the kaiser's telegram of congratulations to President Kruger of the Transvaal—a deliberate insult to their country. And they pointed out a disturbing fact: since 1898, when the kaiser had begun to build a navy, Germany had launched more warships than Great Britain.

Living on an industrialized and thickly populated island, the British were in a different situation from the continental Europeans. They had to import most of their needs, including food and to export their manufactured goods. They had to maintain a large merchant fleet, as well as a navy large enough to defend both their merchant ships and their far-flung colonies.

If war came, other nations could obtain supplies by land, but the British could only get theirs by sea. An enemy that could block the sea routes to their ports would at once threaten their ability to wage war and might well starve them into surrender. Control of the waters around Great Britain was a matter of life and death. And so the news that the Germans were building a fleet of modern warships alarmed the British, and they grew even more alarmed as the new German navy grew more powerful. Their leaders, insisting that the British navy have two warships for every one of all other navies combined, announced an ambitious shipbuilding program, and soon the British and the Germans were engaged in a frantic race to build up their navies.

Year after year the race went on, at great expense to the British and German taxpayers. In Great Britain, fear of Germany mounted, until, by 1912, there were few Englishmen who doubted that the Germans would be their enemies if war came. Long before then, however, fear of Germany's might had forced the British to give up their policy of not taking sides in European affairs, and they had made an ally of their old enemy, France.

In 1904, the French recognized that the British were in Egypt to stay, and the British recognized that the French had a right to move into Morocco. The two powers cleared up their other differences and agreed to support each other if an outside power should protest against their actions. This Anglo-French agreement was not a formal alliance, for neither country pledged itself to help the other in case of war. It became known as the *Entente Cordiale,* a French phrase meaning "friendly understanding."

No sooner was the agreement signed than the French tried to get Great Britain and Russia to settle their differences. And, after its defeat by Japan, Russia proved willing. The British, more and more worried about Germany's intentions, were also willing. In 1907, the two powers divided Persia into spheres of influence, Russian in the north and British in the south. This removed the last obstacle to friendly relations, and Great Britain, France, and Russia were joined together in the Triple Entente.

The older Triple Alliance now faced a stronger combination than the Dual Alliance. But the Triple Entente was less tightly knit together than the Triple Alliance, for the British still refused to say that they would go to war for their partners.

The Coming of the Storm

1905-1913

ALREADY HEMMED in on two sides by France and Russia, the Germans were dismayed to see Great Britain join their rivals. They feared that they would be surrounded by unfriendly powers, and they decided to test the Entente Cordiale. They were anxious to find out how strong it was and how far Great Britain would go in backing up its new ally. The place they chose for the showdown was Morocco, where the French, now with the approval of the British, were policing large areas and taking over territory and rights. And so, in March of 1905, a German warship suddenly appeared off the Moroccan port of Tangier. Kaiser Wilhelm came ashore and made a speech, He startled his listeners by declaring that Morocco ought to be an independent country.

When the diplomats of the world heard of this speech they guessed what the kaiser was up to. He did not really care whether or not the French stayed in Morocco. He was simply trying to break up the new understanding between France and Great Britain. Events soon showed that the diplomats were right. Germany summoned the European powers and the United States to a conference, to discuss Morocco's future. The conference met in 1906, in the Spanish city of Algeciras. But instead of supporting Germany, all the powers except Austria-Hungary sided with France. In the end, Germany's attempt to break the Entente only made it stronger. Even before the Algeciras conference was over, French and British Generals and admirals were planning the joint defense of their countries.

In 1911 came a second Moroccan crisis, when the German gunboat *Panther* anchored in the port of Agadir. The Germans said they were merely protecting their interests, but it was soon clear that they intended a kind of international blackmail. They said they would make no more trouble in Morocco if they could have the French Congo. France agreed to give Germany a slice of its huge equatorial colony, and the *Panther* sailed away.

Meanwhile, a series of minor crises had broken out in the Balkans. The Balkan Peninsula, at the southeastern corner of Europe, was mountainous and wild. Its rugged people, mostly poor peasants, yearned to be free, and their struggles against their Austro-Hungarian and Turkish overlords kept the region in a turmoil. The situation in the Balkans at the start of the twentieth century was extremely confused. Although the Ottoman Empire was steadily becoming weaker, it still held a band of territory from Constantinople westward to the Adriatic Sea. South of this band was independent Greece. North of it were Bulgaria—Ottoman in name, but self-governing—and independent Rumania. West of Bulgaria was the landlocked kingdom of Serbia, and west of Serbia the territory of Bosnia-Herzegovina.

This territory, usually called simply Bosnia, supposedly belonged to Turkey, but had been occupied by Austria-Hungary since 1878. And north of Bosnia, within the Austro-Hungarian empire, lay Croatia and Slovenia. The Serbs, Bosnians, Croats, and Slovenes were all Slavs. They spoke one language, with slight differences, although the Serbs and Bosnians used the same written alphabet as the Russians while the Croats and Slovenes used the Roman alphabet of western Europe. With the spread of Pan-Slavism and the growth of national feeling, the four peoples came to think of themselves as one. They called themselves South Slavs, or Yugoslavs.

By 1900, Yugoslav nationalists were convinced that the Austro-Hungarian government would never let them manage their own affairs, and Serbia, which was already independent, became the center of South Slav agitation. Bosnians, Croats, and Slovenes resolved to take their lands out of the empire and join them to Serbia in a large Yugoslav nation, and the whole South Slav region seethed with discontent. Then, in 1908, several important things happened. In Constantinople, the Turkish reformers, called Young Turks, finally broke Abdul Hamid's stranglehold on the ottoman government. And in St. Petersburg, the Tsar's government, its hopes in the Far East ruined by its defeat in the Russo-Japanese war, turned its full attention to Turkey and the Balkans.

On seizing power, the Young Turks forced the aged sultan to call a parliament. Determined

The Coming of the Storm

to keep the Ottoman Empire from crumbling any further, they made sure that delegates from Bosnia and Bulgaria would sit in the new assembly. This worried both the Russians and the Austro-Hungarians. The Russians, as always, wanted Constantinople. The Austro-Hungarians wanted to annex Bosnia outright, and thereby smash the Yugoslavs' hopes for independence. But if the Young Turks succeeded in strengthening the Ottoman Empire, it was plain that Russia would never get Constantinople and Austria-Hungary would never get Bosnia.

And so its two enemies, Russia and Austria-Hungary, secretly plotted to act together against their common enemy, Turkey. They agreed to call a conference of the powers. At the conference, Russia would support Austria-Hungary's grab of Bosnia. In return Austria-Hungary would support Russia's demand that Turkey allow Russian warships to pass freely through the Straits—the Bosporus and the Dardanelles—to the Mediterranean. But, before the conference was called, Austria-Hungary acted on its own and annexed Bosnia. This infuriated the Serbs. It also infuriated the Russian people, who knew nothing of their diplomats' secret deal. All they knew was that their brother Slavs in Bosnia and Serbia had been badly treated by the Austro-Hungarians.

Also in 1908, Bulgaria became fully independent, and the island of Crete, in the Mediterranean, broke away from the Ottoman Empire to join Greece. Russia failed to achieve its aims in Constantinople and the Straits. Its Triple Entente partners, France and Great Britain, refused their support and the international conference was never called.

So passed the first major Balkan crisis, and it left much bitterness behind it. The Turks were embittered by the loss of still more territory. The Russians were embittered by their own failure and the success of their Austro-Hungarian rivals. The Serbs were embittered by the annexation of Bosnia, and South Slav agitation against Austria-Hungary became even more feverish.

In 1911, Italy declared war on the Ottoman Empire, and quickly seized Tripoli, in North Africa, and the Dodecanese Islands, off Turkey itself. Bulgaria, Serbia, and Greece soon joined forces in their own war against Turkey. The Turks were soon defeated, but the Bulgarians demanded more territory than the Serbs would let them have. As a result, the first Balkan War of 1912 was followed by a second one in 1913, when Serbia, Greece, Rumania, and Turkey defeated Bulgaria.

Another source of trouble was Albania, a wild mountainous region on the Adriatic whose people were Moslems. It was a Turkish province, but the Serbs occupied parts of it during both Balkan Wars, and the Greeks also claimed a part of it. Moreover, it had been vaguely promised to Italy in 1878, when the powers had met in Berlin to carve up the Ottoman Empire.

The landlocked Serbs were determined to get Albania because it would give them a seacoast; the Austro-Hungarians were just as determined not to let them have it. The Russians supported the Serbs in their claim. The great powers, however, agreed to set up Albania as an independent kingdom. This kept the Serbs from the sea, and angered both the Serbs and the Russians.

THE ASSASSINATION OF THE ARCHDUKE PLUNGED ALL OF EUROPE INTO WAR.

So ended the second Balkan crisis. It left the Austro-Hungarians exasperated, the Russians humiliated, and the Serbs desperate. The third Balkan crisis would destroy the peace of Europe.

The Storm Breaks
1914

JUNE 28, 1914, was the Feast of Saint Vitus, an important holiday in Sarajevo, the capital of Bosnia. The city was decorated with flags displaying the two-headed eagle of the Austro-Hungarian Empire, and a blazing sun shone down on the throngs of people in the streets. A small procession of four automobiles moved slowly along, making its way toward the city hall. In the second car, wearing a military helmet covered with green feathers, sat the old emperor's heir, Archduke Francis Ferdinand. He was paying a state visit to this province of the empire he would one day inherit. Beside him, shielding herself from the hot sun with a parasol, sat his wife, the Countess Sophie.

Near the Cumuria Bridge, a bomb came hurtling through the air. It missed the archduke and his wife, but exploded in the street, and flying splinters injured some of the archduke's party and a number of bystanders. The procession went on to the city hall, where the archduke shouted at the mayor:

"One comes here for a visit and is received with bombs. Mr. Mayor, what do you say? It's outrageous. All right, now you may speak."

The mayor, who had been in the first car of the procession and had not seen the bombing, read his speech of welcome. The archduke made a little speech in reply. Then, in spite of the danger of another bombing, he decided to go to the hospital and see the injured persons.

Again the four cars set out, but at an intersection the first two made a wrong turn. As the cars stopped to turn around, a young man on the street raised a pistol and fired two shots—one at the archduke and the other at his wife. At first it seemed as if the bullets had missed them, and the cars sped away. Suddenly blood spurted from the archduke's mouth, and the countess slumped in her seat. In a few minutes she was dead, and the archduke died soon after.

The young Bosnian who had fired the shots belonged to a Serbian secret society, and it turned out that several high officials in the Serbian army and government had some knowledge of the assassination plot. Although the world was shocked by the murders, no one expected it would lead to war. After all, there was always "trouble in the Balkans," and this crisis would blow over, as had the others in the past.

But the leaders of Austria-Hungary decided that it was time they stamped out the Yugoslav freedom movement, which was threatening to tear the empire apart. They would do this by clamping down hard on Serbia. They would not, however, annex Serbia; there were already too many troublesome Slavs in the empire. The big question was: would they have the support of Germany? They sent a messenger to Berlin to find out.

The kaiser himself informed the messenger that Austria-Hungary "could depend on the complete support of Germany." Reassured, the Austro-Hungarian leaders sent a stiff note to the Serbian government. They demanded that Serbia put down all propaganda against the empire, and to do this with the help of the empire's police agents who would be stationed in Serbia. They also demanded that their own men be allowed to help hunt down and punish the archduke's murderers. Serbia was given forty-eight hours to reply.

The Serbian leaders immediately telegraphed St. Petersburg. They were counting on Russian support, even to the point of war. Surely, they reasoned, the Russians would not dare back down in this crisis as they had in the past, for fear of losing all of their influence in the Balkans. But before replying, the Russians consulted the French. And the French, terrified of finding themselves alone in a war with mighty Germany, were determined to keep Russia as an ally, and pledged their support to the Russians.

When the Serbs were sure that Russia and France were behind them, they drew up a reply to the Austro-Hungarian note, and delivered it just two minutes before the forty-eight-hour time limit expired. They agreed to some of the demands, but refused to allow Austro-Hungarian police on their soil. Both countries mobilized troops, and on July 28 Austria-Hungary declared war on Serbia.

Russia prepared to defend Serbia by attacking Austria-Hungary, and Russian generals began to assemble troops along the Austro-Hungarian border. Expecting that Germany would soon come to the aid of its partner, they also assembled troops along the German border. The Germans demanded that the Russians withdraw their army. Receiving no reply to their demand, they declared war on Russia on August 1. Then, sure that the French would go to the aid of Russia, they declared war on France on August 3.

From the start of the crisis, Germany had acted in the reckless hope that Great Britain would not come into the war. Britain was still not bound by any military agreement, and as late as August 3 the French did not know for certain that the British would join them.

But the British were bound to the French just the same, especially by naval agreements. To counterbalance the growing German navy, the British had concentrated their warships in the North Sea. By agreement with France, the French fleet was concentrated in the Mediterranean, watching over British interests there while the British fleet watched over French interests in the north. France's north coast was therefore open to attack unless the British navy defended it.

Great Britain's duty to France was clear—so clear that the Germans could not really have failed to see it. But what aroused the British people to fury was Germany's invasion of Belgium. The army which Germany hurled against the French was so huge that part of it had to cross low-lying Belgium to reach France. The Belgians protested, but the Germans brushed their protests aside and marched into the little country, which had not fought a war since its foundation almost a century before.

In Great Britain, sympathy for Belgium swept all other considerations aside, and on August 4, the British declared war on Germany. World War I had begun. Most ordinary Europeans did not want war, although those who had most to

The Storm Breaks

gain and least to lose, such as the Serbs, were more ready to fight than those who had much to lose and little to gain, such as the French and British. Nor was any government really eager for war, although some behaved more recklessly than others. But the alliance system, which arose out of the fear each power felt for its own safety, tended to drag all of them into any quarrel that broke out between any two. And in some countries, notably Germany and Russia, war-minded army officers were powerful enough to block the efforts of civilian officials to keep the peace.

Even these officers might have worked for peace if they could have forseen the kind of war that was coming. But in August of 1914, few people believed that the war would last longer than a few weeks, or, at most, a few months. Still fewer had any idea that millions of men would die—choked by poison gas, riddled by bullets from machine guns and rifles, blown to bits by grenades and shells from enormous cannon—in the most terrible war the world had yet known. It would take four years for the Allies—the Entente powers and the countries that joined them—to defeat Germany, Austria-Hungary, Turkey, and Bulgaria, which were known as the Central Powers.

LORD KITCHENER'S PORTRAIT HELPED RECRUIT MEN FOR THE BRITISH ARMY.

BRITISH WOMEN AIDED THE WAR EFFORT BY WORKING IN MUNITIONS FACTORIES.

Stalemate in the West, Decision in the East

1914-1917

Germany's generals had for some time expected that they would have to fight both France and Russia, and Count Alfred von Schlieffen had devised a battle plan that took this into consideration. The Schlieffen Plan was a good one, and it might well have brought the war to an early end—if General Helmut von Moltke, who succeeded Schlieffen as the German commander, had followed it.

The plan called for the German army to be divided into an eastern force and a western force. Russia, vast and with few good roads or railroads, would need more time than France to bring up its troops; a fairly small German force could therefore hold off the Russians during the first weeks of the war. Meanwhile, a huge German force would invade France and would defeat it in six weeks. Then the victorious German troops in the west would be sent east to join their comrades in a massive thrust against Russia.

The heart of the plan was the strike into France, and at the start of the war, the huge German army in the west was poised along the French and Belgian borders. Its left wing, running north from Switzerland, consisted of only several divisions, each of 15,000 men, but its right wing, farther north, was made up of most of the German foot-soldiers under arms. The army was supposed to move like a gate swinging on a hinge. Its right wing was to advance rapidly across Belgium into northern France, catch the French army on its left, and hurl it back. Caught between the German right and left wings, the French would have to give up or be destroyed.

For the plan to succeed, the right wing had to be very strong. Count Schlieffen, had understood this; his last words before he died were: "Keep the right wing strong." But between 1905 and 1914, Moltke added eight new divisions to the left wing and only one to the right wing.

On August 3, 1914, the 78 German divisions in the west launched an attack against 72 French,

WHITE SEA
NORWAY
SWEDEN
Shetland Is.
Orkney Is.
Bergen
Oslo
Gulf of Bothnia
L. Onega
L. Ladoga
Helsinki
St. Petersburg
Revel
Novgorod
L. Varner
Stockholm
L. Vatter
NORTH SEA
Gotland
Riga
Moscow
UNITED KINGDOM
ENGLAND
DENMARK
Öland
Copenhagen
BALTIC SEA
Bornholm
Dvina R.
Smolensk
Kiel
Hamburg
Konigsberg
Danzig
Minsk
NETHERLANDS
Amsterdam
Rotterdam
Berlin
GERMANY
Warsaw
RUSSIA
Brussels
BELGIUM
Cologne
Elbe R.
Oder R.
Breslau
LUX.
Kiev
Dnieper R.
Paris
Verdun
Nürnberg
Prague
Brno
Rhine R.
Munich
Danube
Vienna
Pressburg
Budapest
Bern
SWITZ.
Lyon
AUSTRIA - HUNGARY
Odessa
Kerch
CRIMEA
Milan
Turin
Po R.
Venice
Trieste
Fiume
Genoa
Sevastopol
RUMANIA
Rhone R.
Belgrade
Bucharest
Marseilles
Sarajevo
Danube R.
BLACK SEA
ITALY
Adriatic Sea
SERBIA
Varna
Corsica
MONTENEGRO
BULGARIA
Sofia
Rome
Constantinople
Bosporus
ALBANIA
Naples
Sardinia
Taranto
Angora
Dardanelles
Cagliari
GREECE
Aegean Sea
OTTOMAN EMPIRE
SEA
Tyrrhenian Sea
Ionian Sea
Smyrna
Palermo
Athens
Sicily
Tunis
TUNISIA
Malta
Crete
Cyprus (Br.)

6 Belgian, and 5 British divisions. The Germans swept forward; the plan seemed to be working like clockwork. Then, in the east, two Russian armies pushed into East Prussia. Moltke became nervous, and on August 26 he withdrew forces from his right wing to reinforce the eastern front. His striking force in France rolled on, but it was weaker than it had been. The French commander, Marshall Joseph Jacques Césaire Joffre, regrouped his French and British forces along the Marne River and he ordered a counterattack.

The Battle of the Marne, fought from September 5 to 12, changed the whole course of the war. The Germans were forced back, and their hope of a quick victory was ended. After the battle came a "rush to the sea," as each side raced north to reach the ports on the English Channel ahead of the other. The Allies reached the ports in time to keep them out of German hands. The Channel ports were vitally needed by the Allies to receive British soldiers and supplies and their capture was an important Allied victory. Although the Germans in the east were scoring spectacular victories over the Russians, these triumphs proved to be less important than the events in the west.

Up to this point the war in the west had been a war of movement; it became a war of position. Two armies, each made up of millions of men, faced each other along a front that ran from Switzerland to the North Sea. They were so evenly matched that neither could push the other back more than a few miles— and then

AT THE BATTLE OF THE MARNE (ABOVE), THE ALLIES HALTED THE GERMAN ADVANCE AND THE EVENLY-MATCHED ARMIES BEGAN FOUR YEARS OF TRENCH WARFARE.

Stalemate in the West, Decision in the East

only by a tremendous effort, and at a terrible cost. In this situation, the defenders had every advantage over the attackers, and both armies dug trenches—long slits in the ground deeper than the height of a standing man. Dugouts, small caves where men could sleep or eat, branched out from the trenches, which soon extended in parallel rows of zigzag mazes the length of the front. In front of the trenches were strung coils of barbed wire, to entangle enemy soldiers if they attacked. The strip of earth between the German and Allied trenches came to be called No Man's Land.

TRENCH WARFARE

Trench warfare continued in the west from the end of 1914 to the spring of 1918. Both sides were locked in a stalemate, but neither gave up the hope of somehow blasting a hole in the enemy's defenses and pouring through. So the fighting went on, and the method of

FIELD MARSHALL VON HINDENBURG LED THE IMPERIAL GERMAN ARMY IN THE WAR.

1091

GIANT GERMAN RAILWAY GUNS DROPPED OVER TWO HUNDRED EXPLOSIVE SHELLS ON PARIS FROM THEIR HIDDEN EMPLACEMENTS SEVENTY-FIVE MILES AWAY.

attack became as fixed and unchanging as the front itself.

An advance could only be made by concentrating as many men and guns as could be spared from other parts of the front along one short stretch. The attack began with an artillery barrage, which sometimes lasted for days. At the Somme River in 1916, for instance, the Allies placed 2,000 heavy cannon behind a ten-mile front and bombarded the German trenches and gun sites for seven days and nights.

After the barrage infantrymen with rifles and hand grenades clambered out of their trenches and hurried forward at a trot. They wore helmets, and sometimes, if the wind favored an enemy gas attack, gas masks. If the artillery had done its work well, the attacking infantrymen would struggle forward five or ten miles across a nightmare landscape barren of trees, houses, or any other sign of life. But soon they would hear the deadly rattle of enemy machine-gun fire. Some would fall, dead or wounded, and the rest would drop to the ground and dig for cover.

1092

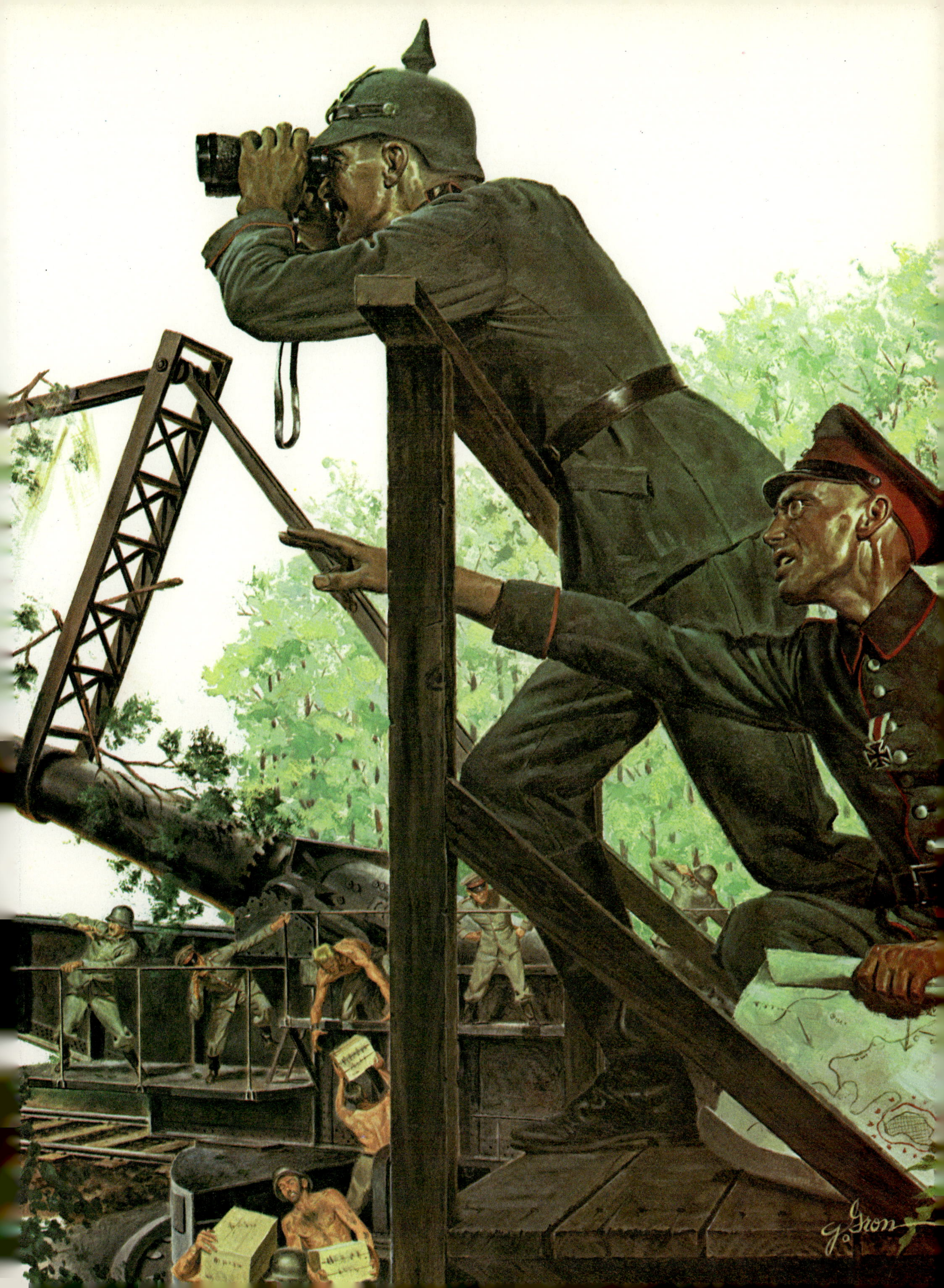
G. Gron

BELOW: THE ORDER TO GO "OVER THE TOP" MEANT LEAVING THE SAFETY OF THE TRENCHES AND CHARGING AGAINST MACHINE-GUNS.

LEFT: "NO MAN'S LAND" WAS THE NAME GIVEN TO THE TERRITORY THAT LAY BETWEEN TWO LINES OF TRENCHES.

Because the big guns could only be moved forward very slowly, the attack was halted.

Machine guns were the greatest killers of the war. Against them, assault was useless, for one well-placed gun could mow down dozens or even hundreds of attackers in minutes. Yet the governments and generals demanded victory, and the attacks went on. Only in the last stage of the war, when the British brought tanks into battle, was a way found to protect men against machine gun bullets.

Never before had the world seen such slaughter. Never had men fought and died in such enormous numbers for such small gains. The "war of position" was as horrifying a chapter as any in human history. In 1915, when the German

RIGHT: IN THE GALLIPOLI CAMPAIGN, RIDERS CARRIED BASKETS OF HOMING PIGEONS FOR IMPORTANT MESSAGES.

THESE BRITISH SOLDIERS WERE BLINDED BY A GAS ATTACK. BOTH SIDES IN THE WAR USED POISON GAS AS A WEAPON.

THE WAR WAS FOUGHT ON MANY FRONTS. THESE AUSTRIAN SKI TROOPS HELPED BLOCK A RUSSIAN ADVANCE IN THE CARPATHIAN MOUNTAINS.

AUSTRIAN SENTRIES IN THE ALPS WERE OFTEN ONLY A FEW HUNDRED YARDS FROM THE ITALIAN LINES ACROSS VALLEYS HALF A MILE DEEP.

GENERAL VON MACKENSEN, THE GERMAN COMMANDER IN POLISH GALICIA.

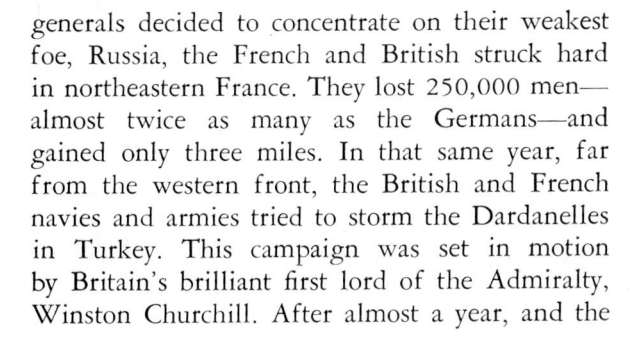

GRAND DUKE NICHOLAS, THE SIX-FOOT-SIX RUSSIAN COMMANDER-IN-CHIEF.

generals decided to concentrate on their weakest foe, Russia, the French and British struck hard in northeastern France. They lost 250,000 men—almost twice as many as the Germans—and gained only three miles. In that same year, far from the western front, the British and French navies and armies tried to storm the Dardanelles in Turkey. This campaign was set in motion by Britain's brilliant first lord of the Admiralty, Winston Churchill. After almost a year, and the loss of 145,000 men killed and wounded, the Allies gave up the attempt.

For 1916, the Allies planned a huge attack along the Somme River. But the Germans struck first, attacking the fortified French city of Verdun in February. With incredible heroism, the French defenders made good their commander's vow that the enemy "shall not pass." Finally the Germans gave up the siege; they had lost 330,000 men, the French 350,000.

THESE AERIAL PHOTOGRAPHS SHOW FORT DOUAUMONT AT VERDUN BEFORE AND AFTER THE GERMAN ARTILLERY BOMBARDMENT, THE HEAVIEST OF THE WAR.

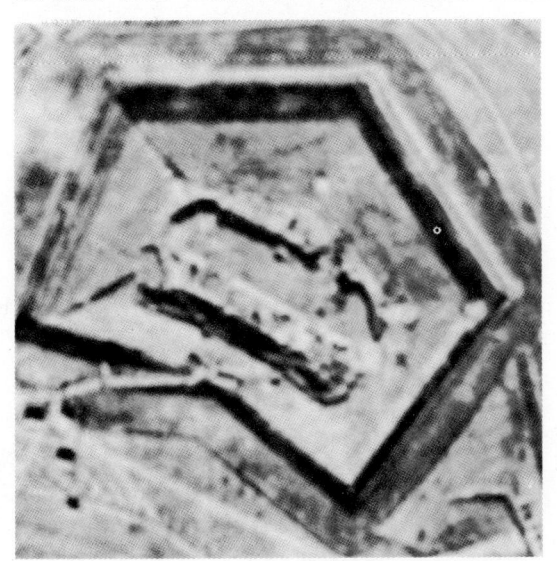

MACHINE GUNS (ABOVE) TOOK A HEAVY TOLL IN LIVES. THE WOUNDED (LEFT) HAD TO BE CARRIED LONG DISTANCES UNDER FIRE TO MEDICAL AID. TAXIS (BELOW) TOOK FRENCH TROOPS TO THE BATTLE OF THE MARNE. THE BRITISH DEVELOPMENT OF TANKS (BELOW RIGHT) CAME TOO LATE TO AFFECT THE WAR.

While the Battle of Verdun was raging, the Allies launched their attack along the Somme. In spite of the heaviest and most prolonged artillery bombardment on record, the British lost 60,000 men the first day. In a week they advanced only a mile, in a month, only two and a half miles. The Battle of the Somme, lasting from July to October, cost the Germans 500,000 men, and neither side gained anything of value.

Meanwhile, Italy had been bargaining with both sides. In 1915, after winning a promise from the Allies of new territories in Europe and Africa, it deserted its Triple Alliance partners and entered the war on the side of the Allies. The following year, the Italians held off Austro-Hungarian attacks. But Germany and Austria-Hungary overran Serbia and Rumania. Rumania had chosen to fight with the Allies.

Stalemate in the West, Decision in the East

And so the Allies were stalemated in the west and the south, and had been routed in the Balkans. Still, they could point to one area of success—the high seas. Since the start of hostilities, Great Britain and Germany had each tried to blockade the other with their navies. The British had relied on their more numerous surface warships, the Germans increasingly on their submarines, which were known as underseaboats, or U-boats. In this contest, the British had steadily gained over the Germans. Finally, in May, 1916, the struggle for control of the seas was decided off the coast of Denmark, in the Battle of Jutland. For several hours, the entire British Grand Fleet of 151 ships hammered the German High Seas Fleet with its guns. At last the Germans withdrew. They had lost fewer ships and men than the British, but they dared not risk another encounter. The German fleet never again left port, and the British, by turning back ships bound for Germany and its neighbors, continued to sap the enemy's strength.

In the remaining area of fighting, the east,

INCOMPETENCE AND CORRUPTION LEFT THE RUSSIAN ARMY POORLY EQUIPPED.

conditions were utterly unlike those in the west. As a result, the war itself was different. There, a highly trained German army faced a horde of Russian soldiers along a shifting front more than a thousand miles long between the Baltic Sea and the Black Sea. Although the Russians greatly outnumbered the Germans, they were no match for them. Most of the Russian soldiers were poor peasants who had no wish to die for their feared and hated tsar or their aristocratic officers, who looked on them with contempt. Furthermore, Russia had little industry and its supply corps was scandalously corrupt and incompetent. The result was that the army was short of cannon, rifles, and almost everything else it needed. In at least one battle, thousands of soldiers went into combat armed only with sticks.

In 1915, after receiving reinforcements from the western front, the Germans took the offensive. Russia's peasant soldiers fought bravely to defend "Mother Russia," but that year they lost about two million men and many thousands of square miles of territory. The following year, during the Battle of the Somme, the Russians counterattacked. Although they took a heavy toll of the enemy, who lost 400,000 men, they themselves lost another million men.

THE EASTERN FRONT

Then, in March of 1917, troops in St. Petersburg mutinied, and revolution swept the country. The tsar gave up his throne, and the government was taken over by a group of liberals from the aristocracy and the middle class. The new government decided to continue the war, and in July ordered the army to launch a fresh attack. But the soldiers had had enough, and the attack bogged down.

GERMAN U-BOATS WERE A CONSTANT MENACE TO ALLIED SHIPS.

A TORPEDOED AMERICAN MERCHANT SHIP

things which we have always carried nearest our heart—for democracy, for the rights and liberties of small nations, for a universal domination of right by such a concert of free peoples as shall bring peace and safety to all nations and make the world itself at last free." Congress acclaimed his speech, and by April 6 both the Senate and the House had approved his declaration of war.

The Allies were jubilant at the news. But the British leaders in London knew that German U-boats were sinking so many ships that England's stock of food was dwindling fast. And, before long, there was only enough food left to last six weeks. Working day and night, British scientists developed means of combatting submarines—hydrophones, which detected the sound of approaching submarines, and depth charges, which exploded under water. Naval officers devised ways of spotting submarines from aircraft and protecting harbors with underwater "fences" of mines set to go off on contact.

578,000 tons; in April, 874,000 tons. Six American ships were sunk in February and March, carrying 48 men to their death, and American public opinion began to turn against Germany.

British agents in America worked harder than ever, and they turned over to Wilson a message their Intelligence Service had intercepted. The message was from German Foreign Secretary Zimmerman to the German ambassador in Mexico. If the United States entered the war, the ambassador was to try to win over Mexico with the promise of territory in Arizona, New Mexico, and Texas.

Americans were outraged by what became known as the Zimmerman message. The war in Europe suddenly seemed a clear-cut contest between good and evil. Besides, American business interests had large investments in England—investments which would be lost if Britain were defeated. And so Americans strongly supported Wilson when, on April 2, he asked Congress to declare war on the Central Powers. "The world," he said, "must be made safe for democracy." The United States would fight "for the

THE U.S. NAVY MADE PLANS TO SEND HUGE CONVOYS OF SHIPS (ABOVE) TO EUROPE EVEN AS PRESIDENT WILSON (BELOW) WAS GIVING HIS WAR ADDRESS TO CONGRESS.

The United States and Victory

AMERICA WAS ONLY GRADUALLY FORCED INTO THE WAR. WILSON'S SLOGAN IN THE 1916 CAMPAIGN (LEFT) WAS "HE KEPT US OUT OF WAR." MEANWHILE, MANY GERMAN-AMERICANS RAISED MONEY FOR GERMAN WAR RELIEF (RIGHT).

The best defense against the submarine proved to be the convoy. A hundred or more freighters, moving together, could be protected if they were surrounded by enough warships to keep submarines at bay. Unlike the United States army, the United States navy was large and ready for combat. It provided sufficient extra warships to make anti-submarine measures effective. By the end of 1917, the U-boats were more of a nuisance than a menace.

In the United States, most Americans enthusiastically aided the war effort. While civilian boards began to draft men for army service, tens of thousands of eager volunteers hurried to enlist. Artists designed recruiting posters. Composers turned out popular songs with war themes. Famous stars of the stage and motion pictures, appearing before huge throngs, urged the public to help the Allies by buying "Liberty Bonds." Shipyards and munitions factories hummed, and women took their places beside men at the machines. In hastily-constructed camps across the land, young men fresh from country farms and city streets drilled, charged at dummies

1106

The United States and Victory

WHEN WAR CAME, WOMEN TOOK JOBS IN FACTORIES TO HELP THE WAR EFFORT.

UNTIL WILSON'S DECLARATION, MANY ORGANIZATIONS OPPOSED ENTERING THE WAR (BELOW), BUT SOON RECRUITING POSTERS (RIGHT) COVERED THE NATION.

I WANT YOU FOR U.S. ARMY
NEAREST RECRUITING STATION

ATRIOTS KEEP COOL

LEFT: SECRETARY OF WAR BAKER DREW THE FIRST NUMBER FOR THE DRAFT.

with leveled bayonets, and learned to fire rifles, machine guns, and light, movable field pieces called howitzers.

While the Americans prepared to fight, the French and British held the line on the western front. The French, who had done most of the fighting and had suffered terrible losses, were near collapse. A general named Robert Georges Nivelle, who still believed that a breakthrough was possible, ordered an attack, but the operation was a total failure. So many French soldiers were

BELOW: REGIMENTS OF VOLUNTEERS WERE FORMED IN CITIES ACROSS THE NATION.

AMERICA WAS FAR FROM READY FOR WAR. NEW SOLDIERS HAD TO BE TRAINED ON WOODEN MODELS OF THE WEAPONS THEY WOULD BE USING.

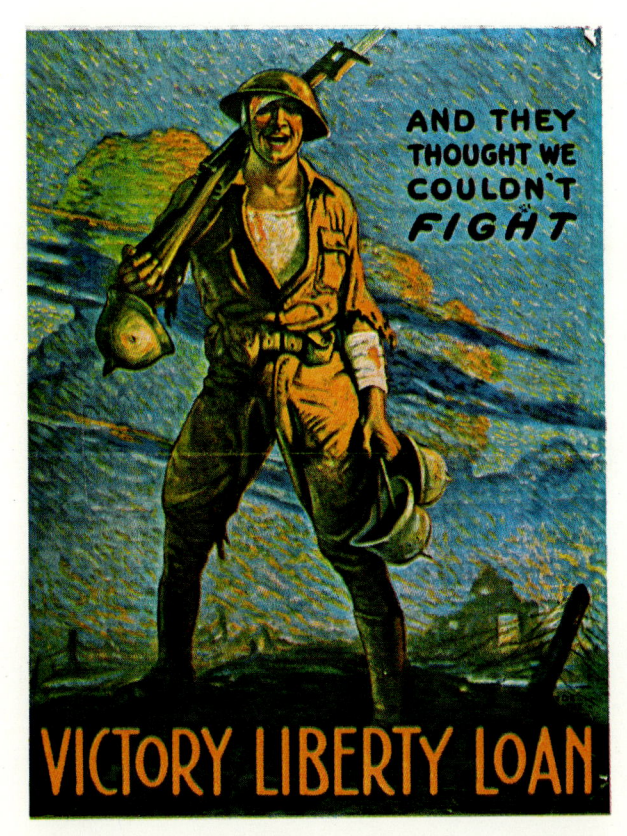

ABOVE: A COLORFUL WAR BOND POSTER

GENERAL PERSHING, COMMANDER OF THE AMERICAN ARMY, WAS GREETED WARMLY BY A FRENCH WELCOMING COMMITTEE.

At the very end of the year they staged an attack with 380 tanks, taking the Germans by surprise. The tanks pushed deep into German-held territory, but had to retreat for lack of infantrymen to hold the territory.

Meanwhile, in the south, Austro-Hungarian and German troops overwhelmed the Italians at Caporetto. They poured into northern Italy, where the Italians, with British and French help, finally checked them. And so the stalemate in Europe continued. Both sides waited, one hopefully, the other fearfully, to see what would happen when the American troops arrived.

GERMANS ON THE BANK OF THE MARNE

THE LAST GAMBLE

In the spring of 1918, the Germans, having won the war in the east, decided on a last desperate gamble. They launched a massive attack, the greatest of the entire war, hoping to overwhelm the French and British before the Americans came to their aid. In March, German troops swarmed over the Allied trenches and charged 41 miles until exhaustion and lack of supplies forced them to stop. They attacked again in April, May, June, and July. By July 15 they were on the Marne River, only 37 miles from Paris.

killed that mutiny spread through the army. General Henri Pétain, the defender of Verdun, relieved Nivelle and restored morale. But he said no more about an attack. "I am waiting," he announced, "for the Americans and the tanks."

After that, the British carried the heaviest burden. Late in 1917, they fought the Battle of Passchendaele, which lasted three months. They lost 400,000 men and advanced only five miles.

THE BRITISH TRENCHES AT PASSCHENDAELE BECAME A MORASS OF SHELL CRATERS.

The United States and Victory

WORLD WAR I ACES MANFRED VON RICHTHOFEN, EDDIE RICKENBACKER, RENE FONCK

There were now nine American divisions in the Allied line. Marshal Foch, the Frenchman who had recently been named Allied comander-in-chief, used them to spearhead a counterattack and on July 18, the Germans began to falter. More than 250,000 fresh American troops were now landing in France each month, and they were rushed to the front. In August, some 354 British tanks rolled over German barbed wire, machine guns, and trenches, smashing the defenders' lines. In September, the Allies opened a gigantic offensive, with American troops in the eastern wing of the attack.

This was more than the badly overstrained German forces could take, and late that month the High Command notified its government that it could not win the war. An armistice, or cease-fire, was arranged, and at 11 A.M. on November

AMERICAN TROOPS GAVE A NEEDED BOOST TO THE ALLIED OFFENSIVE OF 1918.

ABOVE: AN ENTIRE GENERATION OF THE YOUTH OF EUROPE DIED IN THE WAR.

ABOVE: THE FERTILE ORCHARDS AND FARMS OF FLANDERS AND FRANCE WERE TURNED INTO SWAMPS OF SHELL-HOLES.

the war news in the newspapers, playing down defeats and emphasizing victories. To stir the people to greater effort, they spread propaganda, even inventing stories about the enemy's cruelty. The British, for example, reported that Germans had cut off the hands of Belgian children. The Germans pictured the British as monsters who were deliberately letting German babies die by cutting off the supply of milk with their blockade.

When the war ended, people waited for life to return to normal. But what could be called normal? The war had toppled some once mighty rulers from their thrones, and had made the United States into a great world power. It had thrown different social classes together, and had broken down standards of morals and behavior. The past began to seem like a time of stability, when people respected authority and believed in progress. Now they distrusted authority and questioned the old ideals. But one thing was certain—the world had changed and would never be the same again.

LEFT: ONLY THE CHARRED TRUNKS OF TREES PLANTED BY NAPOLEON SURVIVED.

BELOW: GREAT HISTORICAL MONUMENTS LIKE THE CLOTH HALL OF YPRES, BELGIUM, BECAME HEAPS OF RUBBLE.

ABOVE: THE PEOPLE OF EUROPE TRIED TO SURVIVE IN A WORLD WHERE HUNGER AND STARVATION HAD BECOME COMMON.

The Victors Reconstruct Europe

1918-1919

IN THE closing weeks of the war, the Austro-Hungarian Empire came apart. Its subject peoples proclaimed their independence, through "national councils" set up in Paris and London. On November 12, 1918, the last of the Hapsburg emperors, Charles I, abdicated, and the next day Austria became a republic. Hungary became a republic a week later. Yugoslavia and Czechoslovakia also came into existence, and Rumania helped itself to the slice of Hapsburg territory called Transylvania. Before any peace conference could meet, the empire's former subjects had redrawn the map to suit themselves, and the Allies formally recognized the new nations.

THE KAISER ABDICATES

Unlike its ally, the German Empire held firm almost to the end. Earlier in the war, the liberals, democrats, and socialists in the Reichstag, Germany's legislative body, had put off their demands for the sake of national unity. Power had become concentrated in the hands of the generals, led by General Ludendorff.

On September 29, 1918, Ludendorff told the Kaiser that Germany must sue for peace. Furthermore, he urged the immediate formation of a new government along democratic lines, based on the important parties in the Reichstag. The kaiser was astonished. But he soon realized that the army must be in a desperate situation for Ludendorff to suggest such a step. He knew, too, that the proud military aristocrats who commanded the army could not bring themselves to surrender; the task must be left to civilians.

Sadly the kaiser gave his consent, and Prince Max of Baden, a liberal nobleman, agreed to head a cabinet that included the socialists. By October it had put through a number of reforms, but the socialists were not satisfied. They threatened to quit the government unless the kaiser abdicated. Meanwhile, as word spread of the disastrous military situation, the German people began to look upon the kaiser as an obstacle to peace. So did the army officers, who wanted the fighting stopped before the army broke down completely.

The result was that on November 9 Prince Max told the kaiser that he must give up the throne. "Abdication is a dreadful thing," Prince Max said, "but a government without the socialists would be a worse danger for the country." That very day Kaiser Wilhelm signed the necessary papers and crossed the border into Holland, where he was to live quietly until his death in 1942. He had hardly left Berlin when Germany proclaimed itself a republic. Two days later, the fighting stopped.

THE WEIMAR REPUBLIC

The German republic became known as the Weimar republic, because the national assembly which set it up met in the city of Weimar. And

1116

KING PETER I OF SERBIA FLED INTO EXILE DRIVING HIS OWN TEAM OF OXEN.

so civilians arranged the surrender, and the army officers felt that they had saved their honor. They were as much in favor of peace as anyone, but later the story would arise that the undefeated army had been betrayed by panicky civilians frantic for peace at any price.

With the collapse of the German Empire, the puppet states it had taken from Russia at Brest-Litovsk became independent nations. But none of them had a government that really governed, and the borders between them were vague. As a matter of fact, all Europe east of France and Italy was close to chaos. The money issued by the various countries was almost worthless, and their people were on the verge of starvation. Although conditions in western Europe were somewhat better, they were far from good. To make matters still worse, the winter of 1918-19 was unusually cold. Fuel was scarce, and keeping warm was a problem.

And yet, in spite of cold and hunger, in spite of their grief over the men who had been killed in the war, Europeans hoped for a better world. And, as the year of 1919 began, their hopes centered on one man—Woodrow Wilson, the President of the United States.

THE FOURTEEN POINTS

A year before, in a famous speech, Wilson had listed the aims for which the United States was fighting. There were fourteen of them, and they became widely known as the Fourteen Points. Millions of copies of the Fourteen Points had been dropped from airplanes flying over Germany and Austria-Hungary, and in some instances they had weakened the fighting will of the troops. For Wilson did not seek revenge, and even the enemy could agree with many of his proposals.

The Fourteen Points expressed Wilson's faith in democracy, and were a direct answer to the challenge of Bolshevism. Wilson agreed with the Bolsheviks that only autocratic countries started wars, but he also believed passionately that the only just governments were those based on the consent of the governed. He wanted to create a world of liberal democracies.

Wilson called for an end to secret treaties between nations and secret dealing by diplomats. He demanded "freedom of the seas" for all nations, and asked that all barriers to international trade be removed. He said that all the powers,

1117

The Victors Reconstruct Europe

THE "BIG FOUR" ALLIES MADE MOST OF THE DECISIONS AT VERSAILLES. SEATED FROM LEFT TO RIGHT: ORLANDO, LLOYD GEORGE, CLEMENCEAU, AND WILSON.

victors and vanquished alike, should reduce the size of their armies and navies. They should settle their differences in the colonies fairly, and withdraw their troops from occupied parts of Europe. Wilson insisted that all European peoples govern themselves, and that European boundaries be drawn along national lines. Most important of all, he proposed that an organization of all the world's nations be set up, to prevent war from breaking out again.

Although the Allied governments had made a number of secret agreements among themselves for carving up conquered territory before America entered the war, they finally accepted most of Wilson's proposals. But France and Great Britain had objections. The French insisted that a statement be added about Germany paying war damages, and the British balked at "freedom of the seas." With these reservations, the Allies were ready to follow Wilson's lead.

THE PEACE OF PARIS

In January of 1919, Wilson came to Europe for the peace conference and visited the capitals of England, France, and Italy. His tour was a tremendous personal triumph. Wherever he went, huge crowds turned out to cheer him, and several times he was almost mobbed. The feelings of all Europe seemed summed up in a sign strung up in Paris: "Honor to Wilson the Just." For here was something new in history— the head of a great power that had been victorious in war was bringing forth a master plan for peace. Wilson seemed more than a great statesman; he was a savior who was leading the world into a new era.

Later that month, representatives of twenty-seven nations met in Paris to work out the details of the peace treaties. During 1919 and 1920, five treaties would be signed—the Treaty of St.

Germain with Austria, of Trianon with Hungary, of Neuilly with Bulgaria, of Sèvres with Turkey, and, most important of all, the Treaty of Versailles with Germany. These five treaties made up the Peace of Paris.

As the conference went on, it became clear that the actual decisions would be left to the heads of the Allied nations—President Wilson, Prime Minister Lloyd George of Great Britain, Premier Georges Clemenceau of France, and Prime Minister Vittorio Orlando of Italy. The "Big Four," as they were called, were men of different backgrounds—and different ideas. Wilson, a former professor and college president, was an idealist, but he had little first-hand knowledge of any people except Americans. Lloyd George was a brilliant politician who had made a reputation as a reformer, but he had left the conduct of foreign affairs to others. Furthermore, he had promised to "make Germany pay the whole cost of the war."

The aged Clemenceau, who was known as the "Tiger," was a fierce patriot whose only concern was to get the best possible bargain for France. As a practical man, he did not think too highly of Wilson's idealism. He once told a friend, "Moses gave us ten commandments, and we broke them. Wilson gives us fourteen—we'll see." Orlando, who was also a former professor, was interested only in seeing that Italy was rewarded for its part in the war by being given new territories. As it turned out, he was disappointed; Italy's claims were not allowed.

THE VERSAILLES TREATY

Wilson fought hard for the establishment of a League of Nations, a permanent international body to settle disputes between nations and keep the peace. The other members of the Big Four doubted that such an organization was practical, but they gave in to Wilson and the charter of the League was written into the Treaty of Versailles. In return, however, Wilson had to compromise on a number of matters; to satisfy the demands of one power or another, the Fourteen Points were considerably weakened and watered down. Wilson was unhappy about this, but he felt that once the League of Nations was set up, it would repair any damage that had been done.

The Treaty of Versailles was completed in three months, and parts of it reflected the bitter hatred of the French for their recent foes. France received Alsace-Lorraine, which the Germans had seized in the Franco-Prussian War. France was also to govern the Saar, with its rich coal mines, until 1935, when its inhabitants would vote on whether or not the territory would be returned to Germany. To make sure that Germany lived up to the treaty, Allied troops would occupy the Rhineland, along the Rhine River, for fifteen years.

While the Allies, especially France, feared a revival of German strength, they also feared the new communistic government of Russia. They decided to set up strong buffer states that would serve as a protection against Russia. In assigning territory, the conference tried to carry out Wilson's aim of drawing boundary lines according to the wishes of the inhabitants of each state. But in many places the population was mixed, and the treaty created as many problems as it solved. The new nation of Czechoslovakia, for example, had already set its boundaries so as to include a considerable number of Germans in the Sudeten Mountains. These Sudeten Germans, as they were called, had been subjects of Austria-Hungary, and now they wanted to join Germany. But the Allies were determined not to make Germany larger than it had been before the war. They confirmed the boundaries of the Czechoslovakian republic, leaving the Sudeten Germans unwilling citizens of Czechoslovakia.

Poland, which lay between Russia and Germany, was made a large state. To give it an outlet on the sea, the conference added to it a strip of German territory running north to the Baltic. The "Polish corridor," as this strip was called, cut East Prussia off from the rest of Germany. Danzig, a German port, was made a free city that belonged to no country.

Under another provision of the treaty, Germany lost all its colonies. But instead of letting them be taken over directly by the Allies, Wilson and a South African leader, General Jan Smuts, came up with another plan. The colonies were awarded to the League of Nations, which was to turn them over for administration to one power or another. In this way, France and Great Britain got the best of Germany's African colonies, while the Union of South Africa received German Southwest Africa. Italy got nothing.

In the Pacific, Japan had gone to war on the

The Victors Reconstruct Europe

Allied side in 1914, hoping to seize islands held by Germany. The treaty gave Japan the right to administer former German possessions north of the equator, while Australia and New Zealand divided those south of the equator. Japan claimed the German leaseholds and sphere of influence in China, but China demanded an end to all foreign rights on its territory. A compromise gave the Japanese half of what they asked for—and left the Japanese unsatisfied and the Chinese outraged.

SCAPA FLOW

The Allies took over the German fleet, now assembled in Scapa Flow, north of Scotland. But before British seamen could board the warships, their German crews deliberately sank them all. And so the Germans could say that their navy, like their army, never actually surrendered.

The postwar German army was limited to 100,000 men, and the treaty forbade the Germans to have heavy artillery, airplanes, or submarines. Germany was not allowed to draft civilians for military training or to maintain a reserve. The result was that the German army became completely professional, and its officers had at least as much prestige as ever.

The war in the west had been fought entirely on the soil of France and Belgium. Both countries had suffered huge losses of life and property, and they demanded that Germany pay for them. At the conference, their governments submitted staggering bills. The Belgians claimed that Germany should pay them a sum larger than the entire wealth of all Belgium. The French and the British wanted Germany to pay every penny the war had cost them. Wilson pointed out that Germany could not possibly raise such vast sums, and even Clemenceau had to agree. "To ask for over a trillion francs," he sighed, "would lead to nothing practical."

The treaty finally stated that Germany must pay war damages, but left it to a future committee to set the exact sum. As a first payment, Germany had to give up most of its merchant fleet, make deliveries of coal, and surrender all property owned by German citizens outside Germany. This last requirement ended Germany's career as an overseas investor.

To justify their demand for war damages, the Allies wrote a special "war guilt" clause into

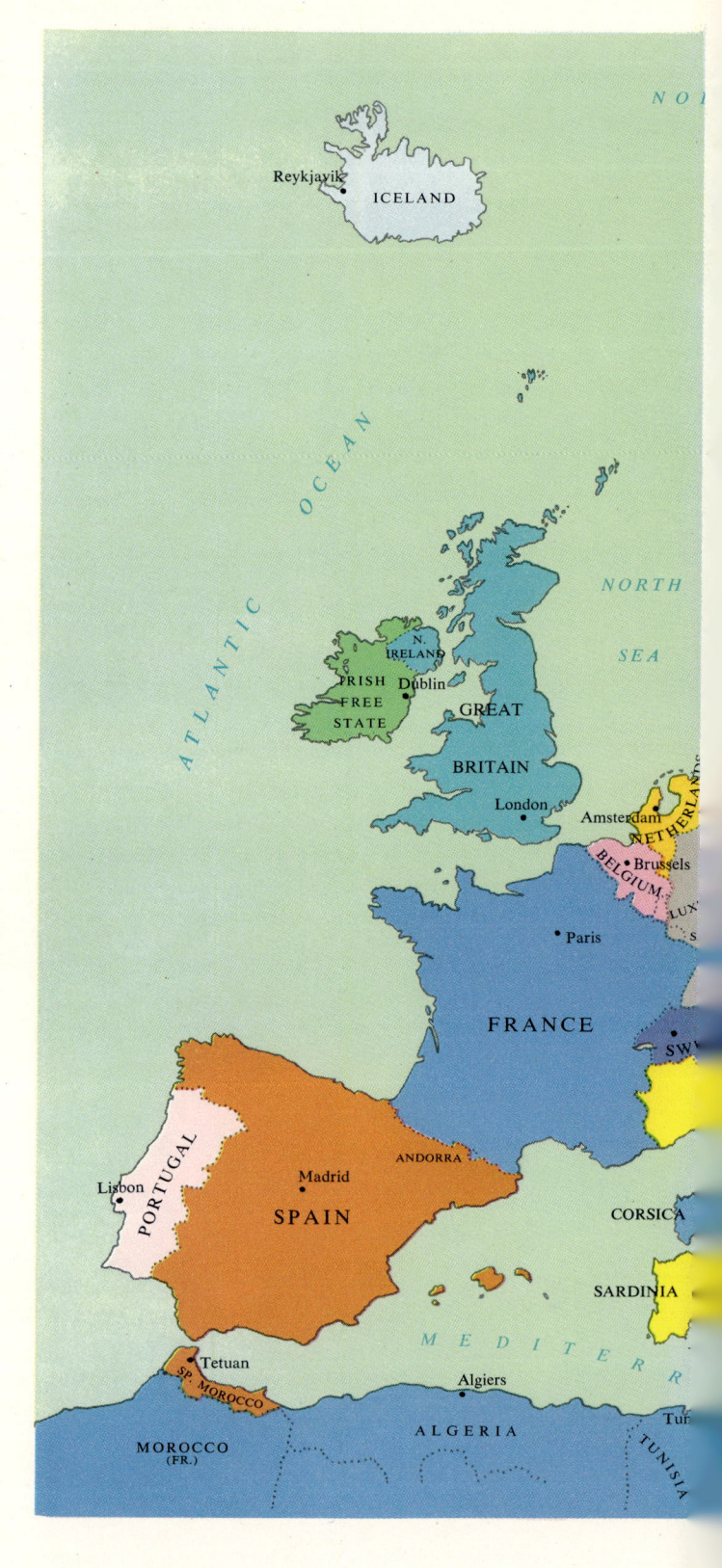

1120

The Victors Reconstruct Europe

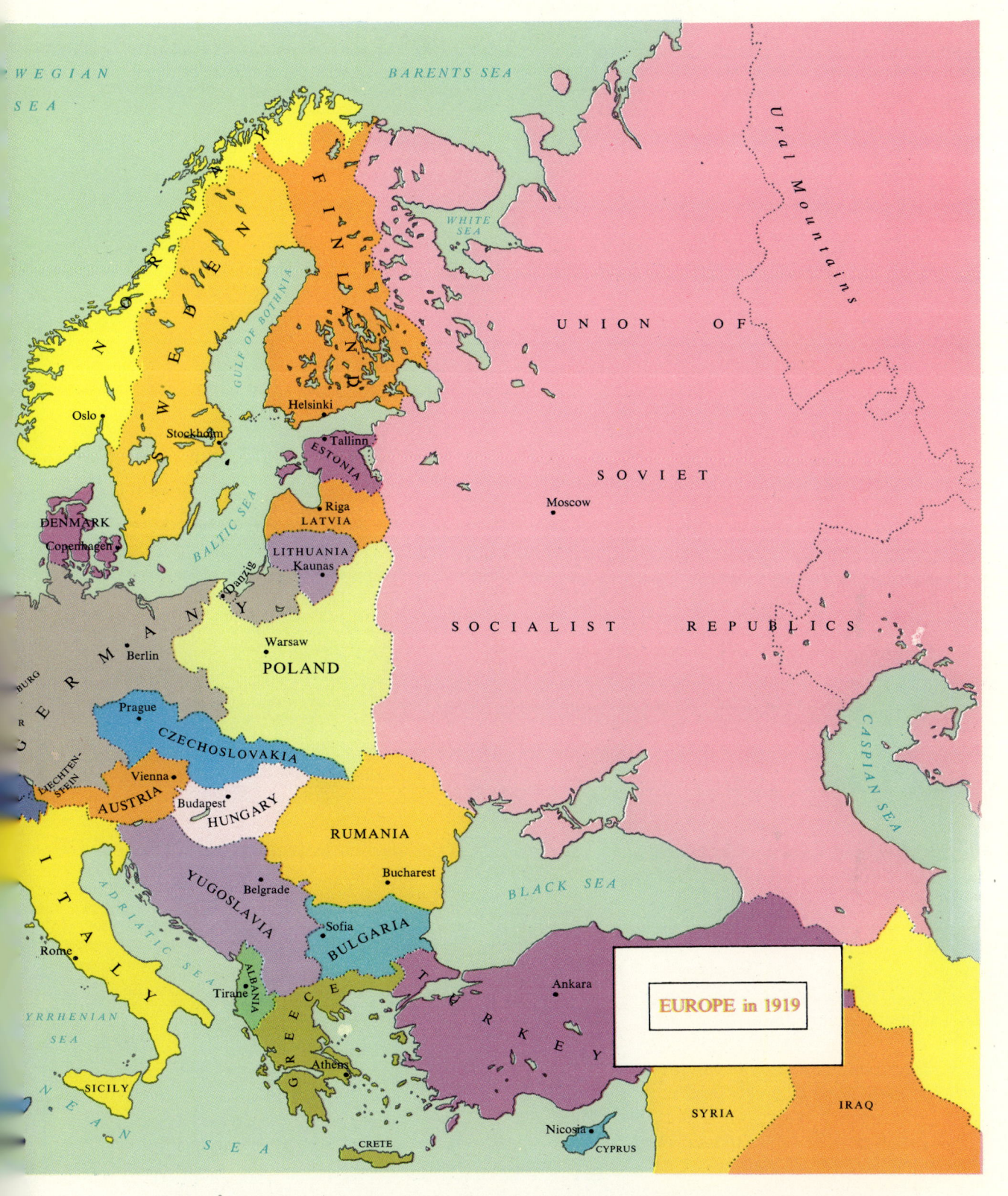

EUROPE in 1919

THE VICTORS AT VERSAILLES REDREW THE MAP OF EUROPE WITH TWO PURPOSES IN MIND: TO WEAKEN GERMANY, AND TO CREATE A BAND OF INDEPENDENT COUNTRIES BETWEEN THE SOVIET UNION AND WESTERN EUROPE.

the treaty. This clause bound Germany to accept the responsibility for all damage and loss resulting from the war. It stated that the war had been "imposed on them [the Allies] by the aggression of Germany and her allies."

When the German people learned of this clause they were indignant. They did not consider themselves responsible for the war, and felt insulted to be asked to accept guilt they did not feel. In May, 1919, when the treaty was presented to the German representatives at Versailles, they refused to sign.

At this, the German government was thrown into a crisis. No German was willing to risk the condemnation of his countrymen by setting his name to such a treaty. But someone had to be found to sign it, and at last a group drawn from two middle-of-the-road political parties agreed to undertake the hateful duty.

In the Hall of Mirrors at Versailles, whose thousands of glittering panels had once reflected the magnificent courts of the French kings, dignitaries from all the Allied nations waited for the Germans to arrive. Two men came in, wearing suits as plain as their names—Mueller and Bell. They looked lonely, almost ashamed. Allowing themselves to be led to a long table, they drew out pens and signed the document which officially ended World War I and unofficially set Germany on a road that would lead to an even more terrible war.

After the Peace of Paris
1919-1920

DURING THE war, three great empires—the Russian, the Austro-Hungarian, and the German—had vanished forever. Then, by the Treaty of Sèvres, a fourth empire, the Ottoman, was quietly put to death. Turkey was confined to Asia Minor and became a republic. Of its former possessions, the League of Nations assigned Syria and Lebanon to France, and Palestine and Iraq to Great Britain. Trans-Jordan and Saudi Arabia, which had fought the Turks under an adventurous British colonel named T. E. Lawrence, became independent kingdoms.

In Europe, there were seven new states: Finland, Estonia, Latvia, Lithuania, Poland, Czechoslovakia, and Yugoslavia. The first six, with Rumania, formed a zone that blocked Russian communism from spreading westward. Rumania had grown larger at the expense of Hungary and Russia, and Greece at the expense of Turkey. Hungary and Austria were made small independent states, with no link between their governments.

The South Slavs, who had triggered the crisis that brought on the war, saw their dream come true in a free, united Yugoslavia. But some Yugoslavs were still dissatisfied, for the Allies, in line with their secret treaty of 1915, had given Italy the port of Trieste and some islands on the Dalmatian coast of the Adriatic. Italy also received the Trentino and South Tyrol, former Austro-Hungarian lands.

AMERICA AND THE LEAGUE

Although the five treaties of the Peace of Paris changed the map of the world, it left more than one nation resentful and discontented. The Italians felt that the Allies had betrayed them by not giving them any of the German colonies. The Japanese felt cheated of their rightful gains in the Pacific. And the Germans were particularly bitter, for they felt they had been unjustly treated in almost every way. When the peace conference began, they had expected that the Allies would treat them with moderation. After all, they had adopted a democratic form of government, in keeping with the wishes of President Wilson. But the German republic had been forced to accept a treaty so harsh that the change of government seemed to have no effect on the Allies; they acted as if they were still dealing with the German Empire.

THE DELEGATES TO THE VERSAILLES CONFERENCE APPROPRIATELY MET IN THE HALL OF MIRRORS, BUILT FOR KING LOUIS XIV, WHO WANTED TO EXTEND HIS POWER OVER ALL OF EUROPE.

LE ROY GOUVERNE

SENATOR HENRY CABOT LODGE

Germany had a tradition of militarism and obedience to authority, rather than a tradition of democracy, and the Treaty of Versailles did nothing to aid the development of German democracy. The German people overlooked the fact that the Republic had had little choice and blamed it for agreeing to the humiliating treaty; the hard times that followed the war added to their dislike and distrust of the government.

Later, the Allies themselves began to have some doubts about the treaty. They saw that some of its provisions, like the demand for huge payments, could not be enforced, and that other provisions, such as the creation of an all-professional army, might lead to results that were the opposite of what they intended.

The United States never formally agreed to the treaty. Wilson could not sign it unless it was ratified by the Senate, and as soon as he came home from the peace conference he worked to win the Senate's support. And, since the treaty contained the charter of the League of Nations, accepting it meant joining the League. At first, many Americans favored this step. But some men in high positions were against it, and among them was Henry Cabot Lodge, the senator from Massachusetts.

Lodge was a Republican, and he had long been opposed to the policies of Wilson, who was a Democrat. In the struggle over the treaty and the League, he had some important advantages. The Republicans outnumbered the Democrats in the Senate, and they had no wish to aid the head of the rival party. Moreover, as chairman of the Senate's Foreign Relations Committee, Lodge could postpone a vote on the treaty until he was sure of his strength—and he did.

WEAKNESS OF THE LEAGUE

As the months passed, Americans began to lose their faith in Wilson's ideals. They were shocked by the sharp bargaining of the Allied leaders in Paris and the weakening of the Fourteen Points. They were disgusted with Europe and its endless quarrels and struggles for power. Perhaps the United States should tend to its own business and let Europe look after itself. Lodge and others who opposed the League played on these feelings, and public opinion began to change in their favor.

But Wilson refused to give up and allow his country to turn away from the great ideals for which he had fought. Although he was sixty-three years old and worn out by the strain of governing the nation through such difficult years, he decided to carry the fight to the people. In spite of the warnings of his doctors, he set out on a cross-country speaking tour. Traveling by train, he spoke day after day, to small groups in small towns and to huge crowds in the cities. Most of the people who heard him were enthusiastic. The newspapers reported that on September 25, in Pueblo, Colorado, "the entire audience arose and cheered for fully ten minutes." But that speech was Wilson's last. He collapsed of

THE GAP IN THE BRIDGE.

THIS CARTOON IN AN ENGLISH HUMOR MAGAZINE RIDICULED THE REFUSAL OF THE U.S. SENATE TO RATIFY THE VERSAILLES TREATY AND JOIN THE LEAGUE

a stroke early the next morning and was taken back to Washington, where for months he lay ill.

In March of 1920 the Versailles Treaty came before the Senate for its final vote; the Republicans had added amendments that would limit America's participation in the League. Even so, a compromise might have saved the situation, but Wilson was a stubborn and determined man who would allow no compromise, especially with Lodge. Now partly recovered, he urged the Senate to reject the treaty because of its crippling amendments. The vote was 49 for the treaty and 35 against, short of the two-thirds majority necessary to ratify it.

Wilson died four years later, and the United States never did become a member of the League. But part of Wilson's dream was realized when, on March 19, 1920, the League was established, with headquarters in the Swiss city of Geneva. The mere existence of an organization for the settling of disputes among nations was a great step forward. Germany was admitted in 1926, and Soviet Russia in 1934. At the same time, the work of the League was hampered by the absence of the United States. Besides, its most powerful members were Britain and France, and they preferred to deal directly with other nations, as they had in the past. As a result, the League remained weak.

The League proved unable to discipline Hitler and Mussolini, and it failed in crises in the Far East. In 1939 it went out of existence, an early victim of World War II. But something of Wilson's idealism lived on, for the League, unsuccessful as it was, prepared the way for an even greater experiment in international cooperation —the United Nations.

1125

IMPORTANT DATES AND EVENTS -

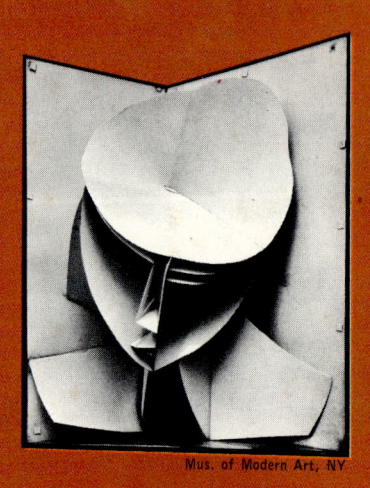

1899 The Boxer Revolt in China is suppressed by the western powers.
1904 War between Russia and Japan; Japan wins and retains Korea; the U.S. helps Panama gain independence from Colombia and begins construction of the Panama Canal.
1905 The kaiser delivers a speech in Morocco, causing a crisis with France.
1907 England joins France and Russia in the Triple Entente.
1908 The Young Turks revolt, restore the Turkish constitution, and begin to modernize Turkey.
1911 A German gunboat arrives in Morocco, causing a severe crisis; France cedes parts of the Congo to Germany; Sun Yat-Sen establishes the Republic of China.
1912 Bulgaria, Serbia, and Greece attack Turkey in the first Balkan War.
1913 Serbia, Greece, Rumania and Turkey attack Bulgaria in the Second Balkan War.
1914 Serbian terrorists assassinate Ferdinand of Austria; Austria attacks Serbia and World War I begins. German armies sweep into

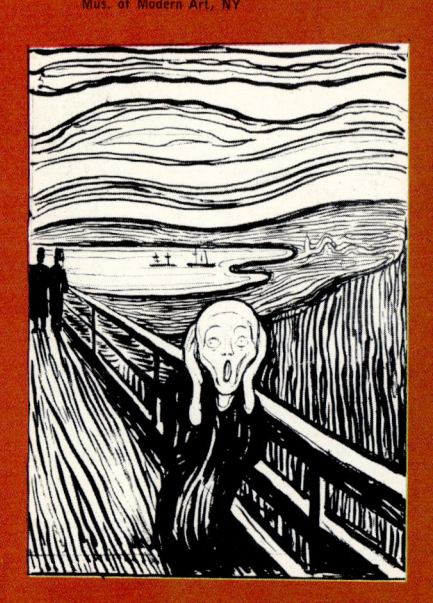

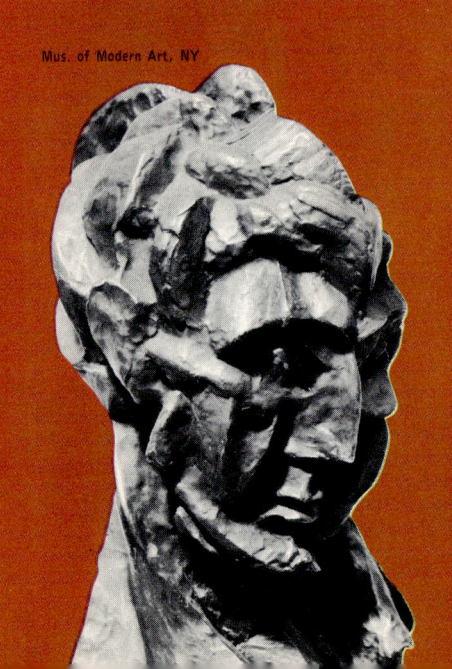

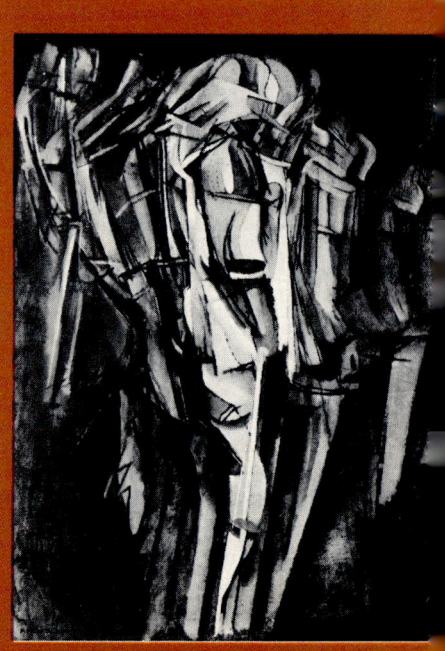

IMPERIALISM AND WORLD WAR I, 1899-1920

France but are forced back at the Marne; trench warfare begins.

1915 Heavy losses on the western front; Italy attacks Austria; America is aroused when a German submarine sinks the *Lusitania*.

1916 Germans attack but fail to capture Verdun; the Allies attack along the Somme and gain 7 miles; the cost of the two engagements is over 1½ million lives; German and British fleets fight the battle of Jutland.

1917 Germany begins unrestricted submarine warfare; the tsar is overthrown; the U.S. enters the war; heavy losses lead to widespread mutinies in the French army; the Bolsheviks take power in Russia and sign an armistice.

1918 Bolshevik Russia makes peace with Germany; the kaiser is overthrown; Germany and the Allies sign an armistice, ending World War I.

1919 The treaty of Versailles; the League of Nations.

1920 The U.S. Senate refuses to ratify the Versailles treaty or join the League of Nations.

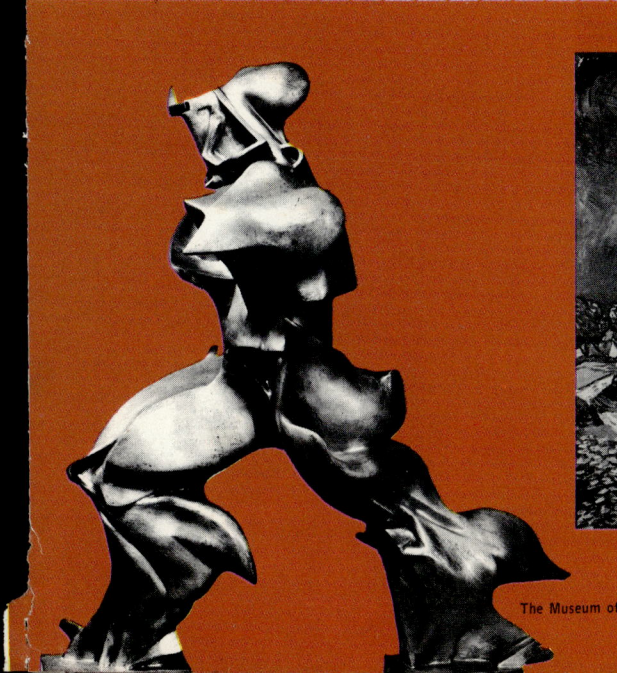

The Museum of Modern Art, N.Y.

The Museum of Modern Art, N.Y.